HELD OVER: "HAROLD and MAUDE" AT THE WESTGATE THEATER

HELD OVER
HAROLD and MAUDE at The Westgate Theater

John Gaspard

Albert's Bridge Books

Second Edition Copyright © 2025 by John Gaspard

All rights reserved. No part of this book may be used or reproduced in any manner whatsoever, including Internet usage, without written permission from the author, except in the case of brief quotations included in critical articles and reviews.

This book contains quotes and excerpts from other sources, all of which are attributed to their respective copyright holders. These materials are used under principles of fair use, with permission where required, or as public domain content. The author asserts no claim of copyright over such third-party materials.

This Second Edition has been expanded and redesigned in 8.5 × 11 format and includes twelve additional production photographs. The text is substantially the same as the First Edition except where noted.

Cover Art, Book Design, and Layout by Author Elevator

CONTENTS

Introduction 1

The Westgate before *Harold and Maude* 9

Harold and Maude before the Westgate 39

Harold and Maude at the Westgate 73

Harold and Maude after the Westgate 103

The Westgate after *Harold and Maude* 117

Coda 139

About the Author 147

Acknowledgements 149

Photo Credits 151

Notes 155

WESTGATE

CYBILL SHEPARD
DAISY MILLER

INTRODUCTION

99¢ ALL SEATS ANYTIME
THE STING

When I was a kid, there were three movie theaters within walking distance of my house: The Boulevard, The Edina, and a tad further away, The Westgate.

If I went to see a movie, it would likely be at one of those theaters.

Although I didn't realize it, we were approaching the end of the era of the neighborhood movie theater.

At that time, most movies started at the downtown theaters and then migrated (sometimes slowly, sometimes quickly, sometimes not at all) out to the neighborhood movie houses. This was in the age just before multiplex theaters (and also before VHS and Home Box Office).

The consequence of this system was that, when a movie went away, it really went away.

It was gone.

Oh, you might possibly see it in a truncated form on television a few years later. But if you didn't take the opportunity to see it when it was in the theaters, it could be a good long while before you ever had the chance to see it again.

With a movie you loved, there was always a sense of urgency: See it now before it's gone.

One movie was an exception to that rule. At least for a while. *Harold and Maude.*

Harold and Maude ran at the Westgate Theater in the Minneapolis suburb of Edina (specifically, the Morningside neighborhood) from March 1972 until June 1974.

Many people loved that movie. They saw it again and again. And they brought their friends.

It sort of made history. It was a unique conflux of the right movie at the right theater at the right time.

I worked for a while at The Westgate Theater, shortly after the *Harold and Maude* years. I suppose my title was usher, but I actually did precious little ushing. I didn't have a flashlight. I didn't take people to their seats.

Instead, I tore tickets. I sold popcorn, candy and a horrible faux-lemonade concoction. I closed the doors to the auditorium when the movie started. I swept up the lobby. And then I opened the doors to the auditorium when the movie was over.

It was not a taxing job. Plus, I got to watch (or at the very least, listen to) a lot of movies.

I'm fuzzy as to my start date, but *Harold and Maude* was gone by the time I was hired at The Westgate. I was hired sometime during the long run of *King of Hearts*, which would put it in late 1974 or early 1975.

I must have worked there sporadically, for in looking at a list of movies that ran at The Westgate, I definitely remember some (*Hearts and Minds*, the odd re-issue of *Where's Poppa?* as *Going Ape*, *The Homecoming*, *92 in the Shade*, *The Apprenticeship of Duddy Kravitz*, *The Magic Flute*) and have no memory of many others. I think I was gone by the summer of 1976, with *Jackson County Jail* probably being the last movie I saw there as an usher.

And a couple years later, like many neighborhood theaters, The Westgate itself was gone.

During the short time I worked there – and the multiple times I saw *Harold and Maude* before that – I wasn't aware of the theater's history.

The building I worked in was tired; the carpet was worn. The lighting was dim. The chairs in the auditorium were the only "new" items in the place (they were actually used theater seats salvaged from The St. Louis Park theater when it had been remodeled years before).

What I never knew was that The Westgate was once a showplace that had had a grand and opulent opening in 1935. That it had a built-in candy store, and an entire wing designed for local meetings and events. That an orchestra once played on its stage. And that the man who founded it was a world-class musician and a bit of a visionary.

None of that was apparent to me in 1975.

What ultimately happened to The Westgate was the same fate which befell other neighborhood theaters, especially once multi-screen competitors began to pop up on the horizon.

The key difference was that this particular theater in a little corner of a first-ring suburb got a tiny bit famous for playing the same movie, night after night, for over two years.

How that all came about is an interesting story. At least to me.

Truth be told, if I wrote this book for anyone, I wrote it for myself to read and enjoy.

But feel free to come along with me for the ride.

An iconic view of Downtown Minneapolis in the early 1970s. All the big movies started downtown.

The WESTGATE before HAROLD and MAUDE

The IDEA

Do we have Carl Fust to thank for the cult status of *Harold and Maude*? It's a bit of a stretch, but an argument could be made. He certainly created the environment for that cult status to begin and grow.

Carl Fust built The Westgate Theater in 1935.

However, music was Carl's first love and – if a good living could have been made from playing first violin in an orchestra – The Westgate Theater might have never existed.

A violinist from childhood, Carl started playing with the Minneapolis Symphony orchestra at age nineteen. After five seasons, he went to London, where he played first violin for the Beecham Symphony Orchestra. He also played for three grand opera seasons at the Royal Opera House in Covent Garden and Drury Lane.

London was also where he met the woman who would become his wife, Constance.

Upon their return to Minneapolis, Carl played with the Minneapolis Symphony Orchestra until 1918. During that time, he

Young Carl and his violin, probably around 1895

Aerial view of the intersections of 44th Street, Sunnyside Road and France Avenue. Carl Fust purchased the empty lot in the lower left corner, between the house and the existing building. The Como-Harriet streetcar line can be seen on the other side of the empty lot across from where the theater will be.

The Minneapolis Symphony Orchestra at the Lyceum Theater in 1917. Carl Fust is in there somewhere.

Carl and Constance in 1921

The Westgate before Harold and Maude

Carl in his pre-London days.

Carl in London, probably around 1910.

Carl Fust with daughters Marjorie and Connie.

also worked as a conductor, directing the orchestra at the Radisson Hotel and at the Lyric theater.

However, having a family to support meant he needed more income, which required a change in occupations. Carl gave up the arts and joined the Montana Life Insurance Company, rising to the position of State Manager for the organization.

But Carl wasn't done with theaters and performing. As a "retirement project," he decided to build a beautiful movie theater not far from their family home in South Minneapolis.

He found a plot of land in the Morningside community, across from the Como-Harriet streetcar line at 44th and France Avenue. Although it was a mere six blocks from the newly erected Edina Theater, Carl felt his theater could withstand the competition.

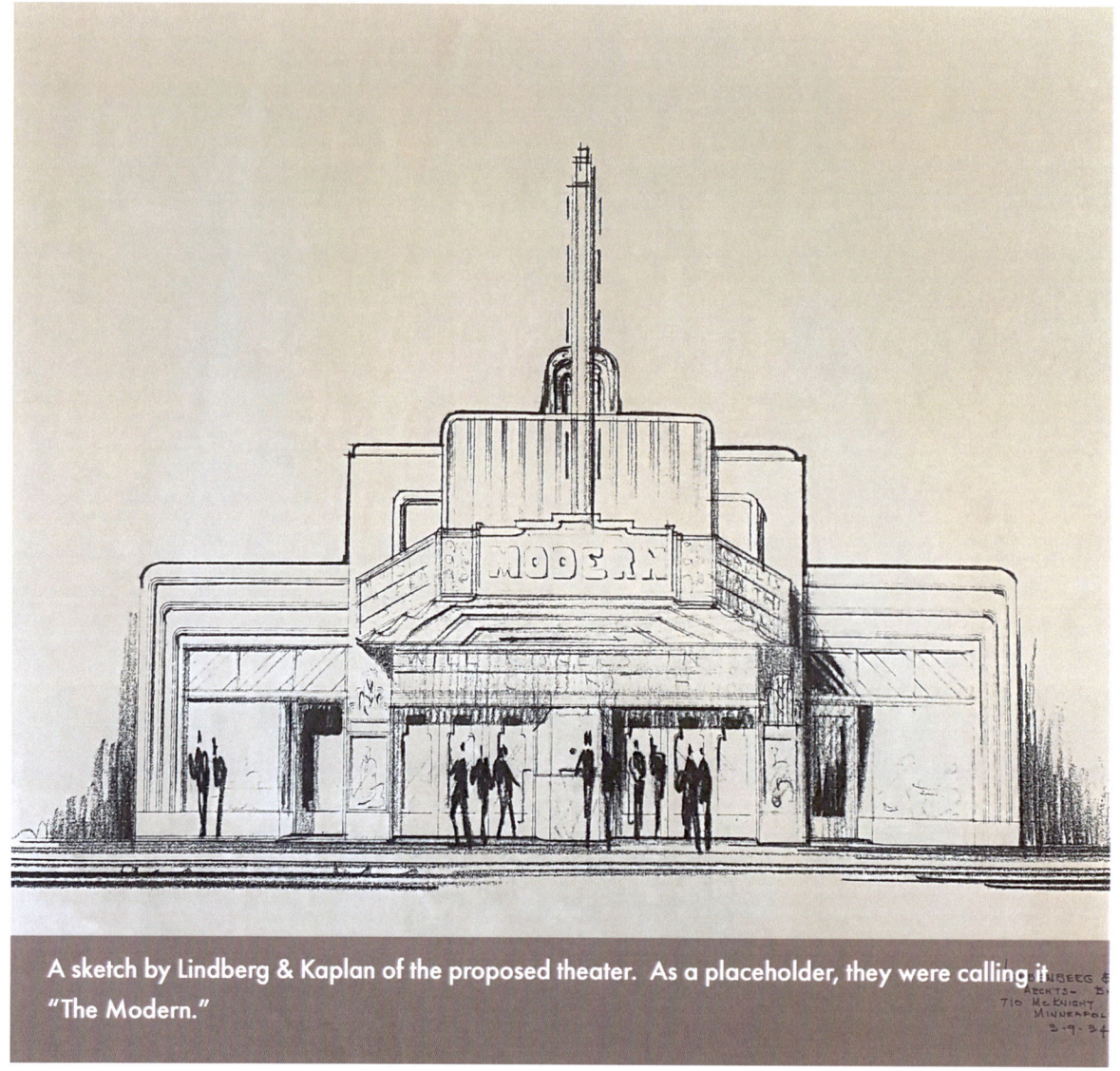

A sketch by Lindberg & Kaplan of the proposed theater. As a placeholder, they were calling it "The Modern."

He commissioned a design from architect Perry Crosier (of the firm Lindbergh and Kaplan). Crosier had also created the streamlined, Art Deco look of The Edina Theater.

Crosier's first design was for a thousand-seat theater, which was rejected by Carl. The architect came back with a smaller and more interesting design, which included a club room/solarium (for meetings, bridge clubs and other small events), a catering kitchen in the basement, and a candy/concession space with its own street entrance.

The design also featured other modern conveniences, such as air conditioning and high-fidelity sound.

Not everyone in Morningside was delighted by the prospect of a neighborhood movie theater.

The Parent and Teacher Association and the Women's Club both came out against it (in their terminology, they "officially expressed their disapproval"). Their objections were presented to the Morningside Council, who declined to issue the necessary permits to

The Westgate before Harold and Maude

In this early incarnation, the screen was set in this position, to create space for performances on the stage. In later years, the screen would be moved a few feet forward.

build and run a movie theater in the Village of Morningside.

Not one to take 'no' for an answer, Carl moved up the chain of command and presented his proposal to the Edina City Council, where it was approved.

At about that same time, local businesses had staged a contest to name the area around 44th and France Avenue. The winner of the naming contest, Mrs. Paul Brown, won $75 for her entry, "Westgate."

Carl now had a name for his retirement project. It would be called The Westgate Theater.

The brand-new lobby. Box office and candy store would be to the left; Club Room would be on the right.

A fairly accurate sketch of how the theater would look, including its final name: The Westgate.

The Opening

The theater opened with considerable hoopla on Friday, November 15, 1935.

An article in the *Minneapolis Journal* – with the headline "Westgate Theater Filled for Opening" – described the event as follows:

The Westgate Theater, Morningside's new amusement center, opened Friday evening to two capacity houses.

Located at Forty-fifth street and France Avenue, the new Westgate, constructed at a cost of approximately $60,000, is the latest addition to Minneapolis' group of better out-lying amusement places. It follows the modern trend in theater construction, and an unusual feature is the large Community Club Room, supplementing the theater itself, and providing

1935 Grand Opening announcement

GRAND OPENING!
of the
WESTGATE THEATRE
AND CLUB ROOM

The Luxury Theatre of the Northwest
45th and France Ave. So.

Friday Night, Nov. 15 at 6:45

Opening Attractions!
1. Special Surprise Number ? ? ?
2. Alice Brady in "Lady Tubbs"
   First Run in Minneapolis
3. Cartoon "Make Believe Revue"
   All in Gorgeous Color
4. Snapshots
   Intimate Glimpses of Hollywood Stars
5. "Lady in Black"
   Musical Comedy Revue With That Marvelous Soprano, Countess Olga Albani
6. Latest News Events

ALL ADMISSIONS 25c OPENING NIGHT
SECOND SHOW AT 9 P. M.

Subsequent Price Policy
Adults 20c to 6:30 - 25c after 6:30. Box office open 6:10 Saturdays, Sundays & Holidays

Adults 20c to 5 P. M.; 25c 5 P. M. Continuous show 2 P. M. to 11 P. M. Children 10c always

FREE PARKING

A unique feature of the theater was the Club Room, which was available for bridge nights and other social events.

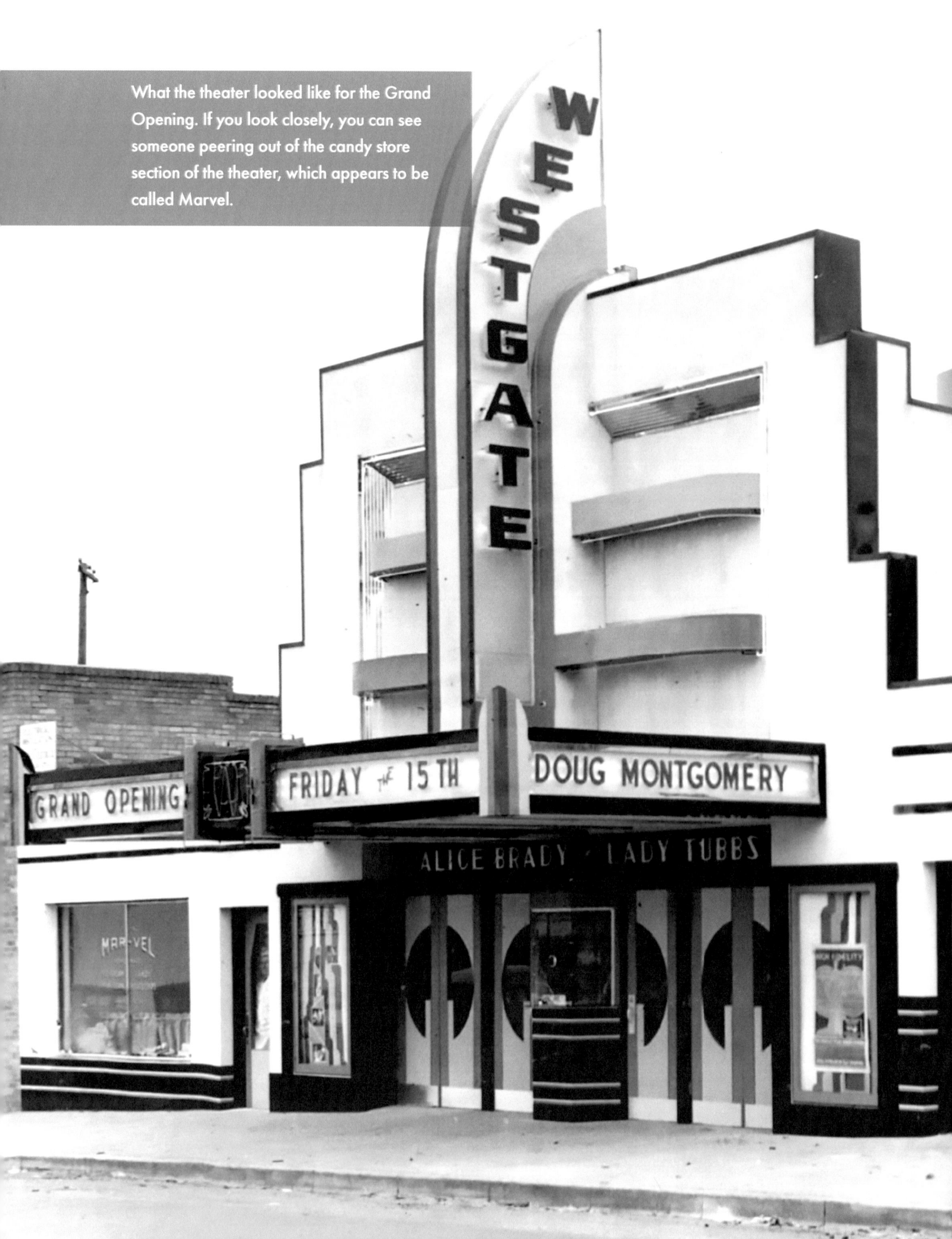

What the theater looked like for the Grand Opening. If you look closely, you can see someone peering out of the candy store section of the theater, which appears to be called Marvel.

Lady Tubbs promotional image, with Alice Brady (right) and Anita Louise.

Lady Tubbs was a first-run feature, something that would be harder and harder for The Westgate to procure.

attractive accommodations for various neighborhood gatherings, such as card parties, club meetings, and other group activities.

The new Westgate was elaborately decorated with flowers for the opening, which was most auspicious. And a special feature of the premiere was the 12-piece orchestra made up of members of the Minneapolis Symphony, under the direction of the new theater's owner, Carl J. Fust, well known in Minneapolis insurance circles.

In addition to the live orchestra, the program included a cartoon (*Make Believe Revue*), a short (*Lady in Black*), a newsreel, and the local premiere of the latest Alice Brady film, *Lady Tubbs*.

Lobby Card for Lady Tubbs, with Alice Brady and Alan Mowbray.

The Make-Believe Revue was a short, animated film produced by Charles Mintz for Columbia Pictures as part of their "Color Rhapsodies" series.

This first-run film had been well-reviewed, with *The New York Times* saying, "In *Lady Tubbs*, Alice Brady comes through handsomely with a performance that at once justifies the picture's inclusion in any list of the season's best comedies.

"Homer Croy's story of Mom Tubbs – the cook in the railroad construction camp who inherits a fortune, assumes a title and surges into Long Island's smart set – has been screened with a shrewd sense of filmic pace, a bright eye for every comic opportunity and, withal, the pleasant quality of being believable.

"This last is all the more welcome considering the number of recent photoplays that have begun as comedies, dropped into farce and wound up as sorry burlesque. But Mom Tubbs, as Miss Brady plays her, is authentic."

Although The Westgate's opening week kicked off with a first-run film, doing that repeatedly turned out to be a larger issue than Carl had anticipated. He simply didn't have access to the biggest and best films.

Which was too bad, as 1935 was a good year for movies, producing such hits as *The Man Who Knew Too Much*, *Bride of*

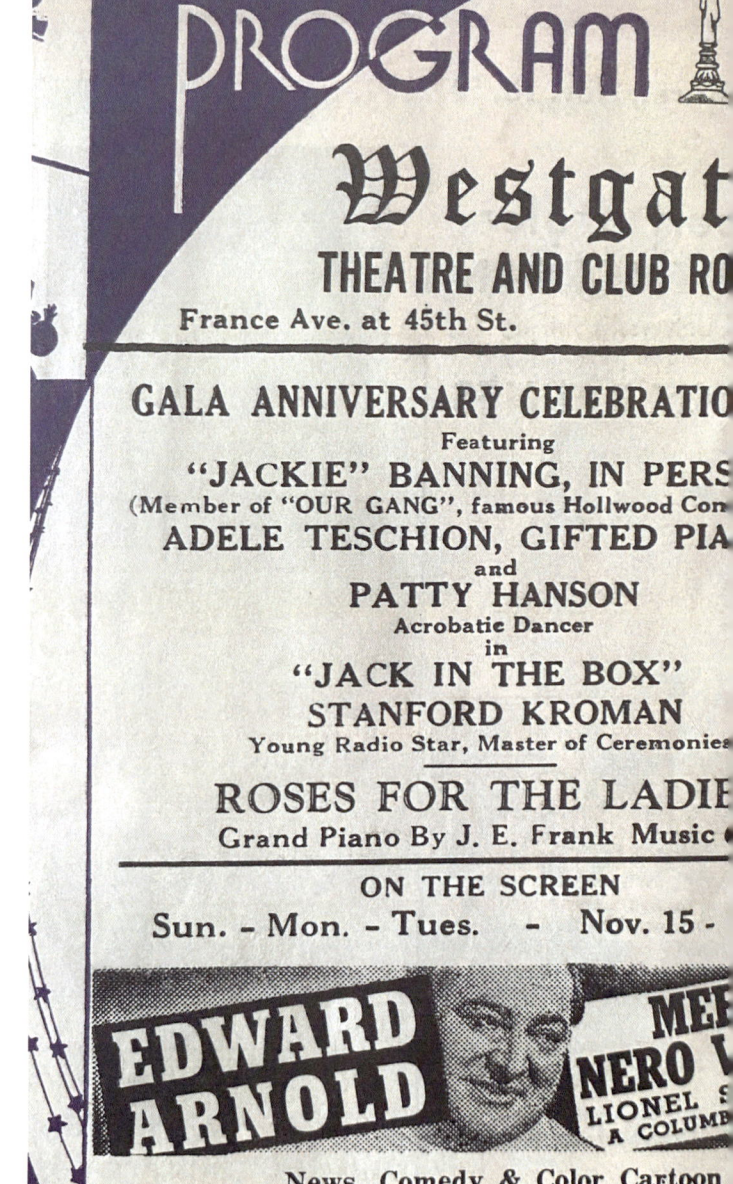

Westgate Theatre To Be Opened Soon

Carl J. Fust, owner of the new Westgate theatre at Sunnyside and France avenues, has announced that the show house will open the latter part of this month. The structure was designed by Perry E. Crosier, well-known theatre architect, who incorporated in his plans some of the most exclusive and distinctive features at the command of his profession. Indirect lighting is provided for exterior and interior, and a spacious club and bridge room, with caterer's service, is available. The interior decorations are modern in color and design, and the air conditioning, projection, high-fidelity wide-range sound and seating are of the latest type. Free parking grounds with walks to the main entrance of the theatre are provided. The theatre is expected to attract residents of the Country Club, Morningside, Edina, Browndale

Theatre To Open Within Four Weeks

Local Manager Promises Newest Features of Cinema World

Within the next four weeks the new West Gate theatre will be opened to the public. Operated by Carl J. Fust, who has had theatrical experience in London and the United States, the cinema house will have the newest features in theatre construction, following the modernistic trend. High range fidelity sound system, modern air conditioning, and ventilating system, large bridge and club room for neighborhood parties and spacious foyer and lobby are among the features, with ample parking space provided.

Lady in Black was directed by Joseph Henabery, one of the most prolific directors of shorts in both the silent and sound eras

But Carl quickly learned that as a single theater, without a larger organization behind him, he simply didn't have access to these first-run movies. The Westgate was relegated to second (and sometimes third) run movies, while more

Frankenstein, The 39 Steps, Top Hat, A Night at the Opera, and *Alice Adams.* Tickets were generally 25 cents and, even in the midst of the depression, many families went to the movies once a week.

THEATER OPENED AT FRANCE & 45TH

One of the interesting features of the new Westgate theater which was recently opened by Carl J. Fust at Forty-fifth street and France is the community club room decorated and furnished in the modern manner made popular by the Chicago Century of Progress. Leather, corduroy, chromium and glass are used to make this room a most attractive meeting place for community groups.

The feature offered in June 1936 – First a Girl – had already been screened all over town (even at the nearby Edina Theater) before The Westgate was able to show it.

popular fare ended up a half a mile away at The Edina Theater.

As time went on, this continued to be an issue for the theater. As his daughter, Marjorie, wrote in her memoir: "Film row was monopolized, so we were unable to get very good pictures. They had a monopoly on the high rated movies, so we were unable to get Fox or MGM and got only so-called "Cluck" pictures; consequently, our attendance was not very good."

What this meant was that The Westgate was only able to present movies that had already played elsewhere in town. Often at several other theaters.

Even at their one-year anniversary – featuring an appearance of a cast member of *Our Gang*, live performances and a radio star host – the feature presented, *Meet Nero Wolfe*, had already opened at The Orpheum in August, and played at other theaters around town before landing at The Westgate.

This same issue continued to plague Carl as the theater moved into 1937.

And then tragedy struck.

The Westgate before Harold and Maude

The TRAGEDY

FROM CARL FUST'S DAUGHTER, Marjorie's, memoir:

"In the fall of 1936, while Daddy was driving across the intersection at Loring Park and Hennepin Avenue, his car was hit broadside by a Franklin Creamery Truck. When he arrived home, mother suspected something was wrong, because his face was so ashen white. He insisted nothing was wrong, but later mother caught him in the bathroom flicking glass away from his glasses and ears. He then admitted what had happened. He seemed to be physically okay, though the car was badly damaged on his side of the car.

"In about March, his knee began to swell up and they conjectured that it had hit the dashboard when the car was hit. And because of his hemophiliac condition, the bleeding internally was causing the swelling.

"He stayed home from work and mother loved to wait on him and tried to nurse him back to good health. He contracted a cold, and his health began to deteriorate so badly that we called the doctor, who ordered an ambulance. He was hospitalized at Eitel Hospital and Dr. Kistler attended him. The doctor said if he lived through that night, he would be out of danger. He was wrong, because Daddy passed away the next morning.

"We were all devastated and shocked, for he was only 47 years of age. How Mummy lived through this loss, I will never know, except that Connie and I were still at home and comforted her as much as we could. I guess it was her British pluck that carried her through."

The Westgate Theater would be forced to move ahead without the imagination and guidance of its founder, Carl Fust.

Perhaps the last photo taken of Carl Fust. (The Rose Gardens in Minneapolis, September 1936)

The WAR YEARS and BEYOND

Soon after Carl Fust's death, ownership of The Westgate was taken over by the owner of The Edina Theater, Martin Stein. But even under new ownership, The Westgate still retained its second-class status when it came to the movies it could offer.

At The Westgate – as an ad for *Citizen Kane* proclaimed – you could see the top film of 1941 … if you didn't mind waiting until 1942 to see it. Many other hit films also turned up at The Westgate, but only after they'd been shown at just about every other theater in town.

The Morningside audiences really didn't seem to mind. As Richard Jamieson, who worked as an usher at The Westgate in the 1940s, recalled: "I will never forget when we showed *Gone with the Wind*. People were standing in long lines waiting to get in. Almost all shows were sold out. What a film!!!"

Another key memory for young Jamieson was the time he accidently put a 'typo' on the marquee: "On one Saturday night at The Westgate, our cashier had just gone home, and I was all alone and guarding the front lobby entrance. I also was outside putting up canopy letters, advertising the next day's feature title. The film was a major John Wayne movie."

The correct spelling on the poster, but not so much on the marquee.

The Westgate before Harold and Maude

The letters Jamieson put on the marquee read: *Tail In The Saddle*.

"It took three days," he recalled, "before someone came into the theater and said, 'It's *Tall In The Saddle*, dumbo.' No one I worked with had noticed (my) creative approach to the canopy sign. We had really good sales for that picture, so the management didn't complain."

*

As the theater moved into the 1950s, a noticeable shift in tone began. This may have occurred, in part, because of the physical changes made to the theater itself.

Concessions were moved from the store space next to the lobby, to a brand-new candy counter in the lobby itself. The store space then transitioned into the Morningside Library.

The Club Room was sectioned off into its own separate building, with a portion of it remaining in The Westgate as a small art gallery just off the theater's lobby.

Along with the remodeling, the theater

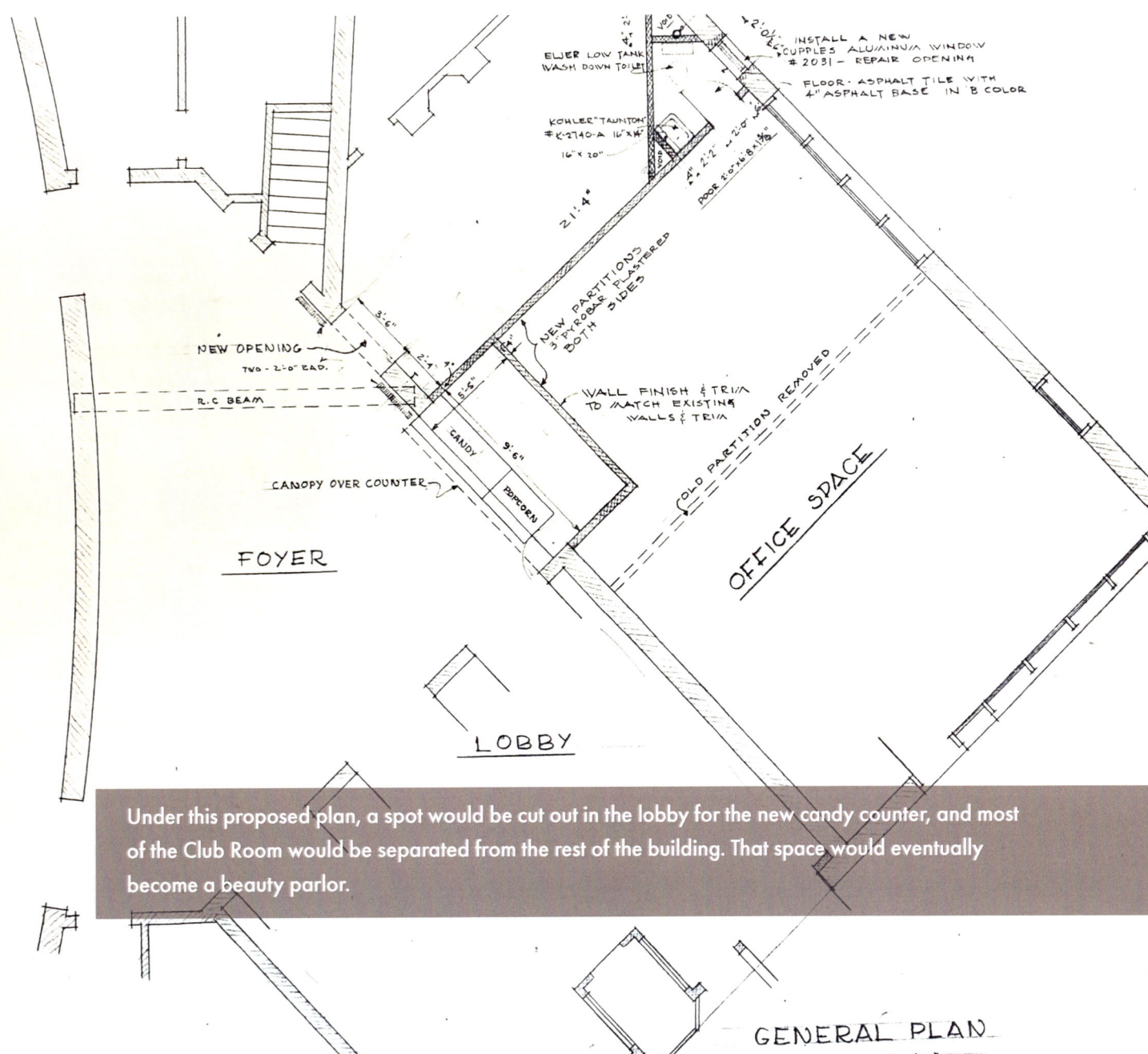

Under this proposed plan, a spot would be cut out in the lobby for the new candy counter, and most of the Club Room would be separated from the rest of the building. That space would eventually become a beauty parlor.

STREET SCENE, water color by Robert Lesch, is included in the score of pictures hung for the grand opening Wednesday of the Westgate Art gallery in the specially remodeled and redecorated lobby of the Westgate theater. Other Twin Cities artists represented in the opening exhibit are David Ratner, Murray Turnbull and Richard Pynn. Keith Havens is director of the Westgate gallery and he plans to change the exhibits at about three-week intervals, with a series of one-man shows and special events. The exhibitions will be on view for all patrons of the Westgate. "Forbidden Games" is the motion picture starting Wednesday.

> The Art Gallery helped to build the sense that The Westgate was the "arty" neighborhood theater, designed to appeal to 'Upper Bohemians.'

changed its advertised name, becoming for several years (although somewhat inconsistently) The Westgate Academy Arts. Mixed in with the traditional fare were "artier" or "adult" pictures.

The theater even advertised a "Swedish speaking" picture at one point, in an advertisement which wasn't even written in English.

The newly designed Westgate Art Gallery featured the work of local artists, further contributing to the "arty" air of the theater.

In fact, *Minneapolis Tribune* columnist Will Jones wrote that he had recently found a term to describe people who patronized theaters like The Westgate: "Theater men have long

The Westgate before Harold and Maude

Se her Skandinaver!
Et levende billede
"EN SOMMER AV LYKSALIGHET"
Fremvises nu i
WESTGATE THEATER
45TH AT FRANCE SOUTH
Der er et helt svensk talende billede
Send ikke barn, det er kun for Mama og Papa

This ad translates as: "Look here Scandinavians! A moving picture, A Summer of Bliss. Now showing at Westgate Theater, 45th at France South. This is a completely Swedish-speaking picture. Don't send children, it's only for Mama and Papa."

considered these customers a breed apart, but there's never been, to my knowledge, a satisfactory name for them. Russell Lynes, an editor of *Harper's*, supplied one in the magazine's February issue: Upper Bohemians."

Jones then went on to quote Lynes on some of the traits of the typical Upper Bohemians: "'Mrs. Upper Bohemian,' wrote Lynes, 'isn't above peeking into Vogue or Harper's Bazaar, though it is usually to complain about what she finds there.'

"Mr. Upper Bohemian, according to Lynes, is likely to be a publisher or editor or lawyer or writer or architect, or less likely, a businessman."

There was one businessman, however, who was definitely interested in The Westgate: Ted Mann, who took over the theater's lease in 1956.

Ted Mann got into the theater business the same time as Carl Fust, when he leased a theater in St. Paul in 1935. At the time he took over The Westgate, Mann was also operating The World and The Suburban World Theaters in Minneapolis.

Under Mann's ownership, the section of the Club Room which had been separated from the theater and become its own building was leased to the new "Lady be Lovely" beauty salon. In addition, he changed the theater's name in some (but not all advertisements), referring to it as The Westgate Playhouse.

Around that time, The Westgate experienced what was possibly their first long run:

TOWN TOPPERS
Here's a Quick Look at:

A CAREER which included a spell as an assistant manager of the Metro theater on the South side—a job which included maintenance, among other things—some time later brought Ted Mann to the ownership of that theater as well as a number of others.

Ted Mann

Once a Diamond Belt finalist in the light-heavyweight boxing division, Mann today is a husky 200-pounder who plays handball religiously to keep his weight at or about that level.

Born in Wishek, N. D., he came here with his parents as a child. His taste of theater business at the Metro led him, in 1936, to buy the Oxford theater in St. Paul and to reopen it.

Three years later he bought the Gem theater in St. Paul and in 1941 built the Oxford bowling center. A year later he acquired the Metro, and a year after that the Royal in St. Paul. In 1944, in partnership with Don Guttmann, he bought the Dickerman circuit of five theaters.

He and Guttmann built the San Pedro and Compton (Calif.) drive-ins, and he is president of the Skyline drive-in theater organization in Duluth, as well as a director of Minnesota Entertainment Enterprises, operating a half dozen drive-ins about the Twin Cities.

In 1945, Mann bought the World and Alvin theaters here. He now has sold all of his theaters except the Duluth drive-in, the World-Alvin combination, and the World in St. Paul. He and Guttmann also operate an industrial banking concern in Los Angeles, Calif.

An occasional golfer, Mann reads biography and politics, is a past president of North Central Allied theater owners. He and Mrs. Mann, with their two daughters, 7 and 12, live at 2731 Dean boulevard.

A short article on Ted Mann in the Minneapolis Star in 1952.

A six-week run was a rare event indeed at any neighborhood theater. It hadn't happened before at The Westgate.

The comedy *How To Murder a Rich Uncle* played at the theater for a remarkable six weeks, foreshadowing several longer runs which would occur a dozen or more years later.

*

The early 1960s kicked off with the first celebrity sighting at The Westgate since the Gala Opening and the One Year Anniversary. Former Morningside resident Tippi Hedren, on a national tour for the movie, *The Birds*, made several stops in Minneapolis, including a visit to her childhood theater, The Westgate.

"I used to go to the movies there every Saturday night, never dreaming I would be on the screen," Miss Hedren told a reporter.

Fun Fact: It would be ten years – almost to the day – before another Hollywood star

The Westgate before Harold and Maude

Tippi Hedren (center) with the guests she invited to an afternoon preview screening of "The Birds" at The Westgate Theater, which had been her neighborhood theater as a child.

would step through the lobby doors at The Westgate!

Now officially part of The Mann Theaters' brand, The Westgate offered an interesting mix of films in the 1960s: some oddball double features (*To Kill a Mockingbird* and *That Touch of Mink* anyone? How about Jacques Tati's *Mon Uncle* and Frank Sinatra in *Ocean's 11*?), many

The Westgate before Harold and Maude

OUR STORY:

Due to the concentrated demand for a relatively small number of commercial films, many excellent and significant motion pictures never reach Minneapolis screens. It is the realization of this "Film Gap" which has led to the birth of the "4 STAR FILM FESTIVAL." We don't pretend the "4 STAR FILM FESTIVAL" is the complete answer, but we believe it is a significant beginning. With the support of you, the moviegoing public, we are hopeful that this series is only the first of many to follow.
— THE MANAGEMENT

"Each Film Is Distinctly Superior And Deserving Of Wider Audience."
— Don Morrison

4 STAR FILM FESTIVAL

Starts Tonight! Color At 7:40 & 9:45

4 Star Film Series Hit Number 2

"I just killed my wife and my mother. I know they'll get me. But before that many more will die."

TARGETS

STARRING BORIS KARLOFF TIM O'KELLY

SUGGESTED FOR MATURE AUDIENCES

NEXT!	COMING!
"THE LONG DAY'S DYING"	"INADMISSIBLE EVIDENCE"

WESTGATE
45TH AND FRANCE SOUTH
922-4666

PARK FREE

The Westgate was starting to build the reputation as being (according to one critic years later) "a sort of nursing home for mistreated films that don't have time to catch on with their true public in the frenzy of normal Downtown first runs and quickie neighborhood runs."

Hollywood hits on their second or third run (*Peyton Place, Guess Who's Coming To Dinner?*), and then the occasional arthouse film (including an Ingmar Bergman festival, prepping Westgate audiences for what was to come with *De Düva*).

This move away from more frequent screenings of arty films (the word "Playhouse" left the logo in the early 60s, so it was once again just The Westgate), was noted by local film critic, Don Morrison.

"I hear the recurring complaint that Minneapolis is cheated of seeing a true cross-section of available films," he wrote in his *Minneapolis Star* column in mid-June 1969.

"Most American movies are exhibited here," he went on. "Also, a major percentage of better-known foreign films, important or modest, receive a showing. But there is a range of other domestic and foreign pictures largely unseen. Some are of special interest or may seem 'forbidding' to the casual movie-goer seeking something meatier on his night out.

"Jim Payne, principal booker for the Mann Theater organization and a movie-booker locally unique for his knowledge and appreciation of quality films off the beaten track, broods about this situation. His latest scheme is a festival of 'neglected' recent movies – high-grade items that have been shunted aside or which have had a poor commercial record for lack of attention."

The Westgate was selected for this four-film experiment, which included Peter Bogdanovich's first feature, *Targets*.

But then the next year, another big change: The sale of The Westgate (and 20 other Mann theaters) to General Cinema Corporation in Boston.

General Cinema already owned more than 200 movie houses around the country and was said to be one of the two largest theater operators in the United States. The company already owned The Edina Theater, which had recently been split into two auditoriums.

Although the Mann management team stayed in place after the sale, most of the films at The Westgate through the year 1970 consisted of traditional second and third-run Hollywood hits, like *True Grit, The Prime of Miss Jean Brodie, Paint Your Wagon, Camelot, Oliver!, Thoroughly Modern Millie* and *Funny Girl*.

And then, in December 1970, Mel Brooks arrived with a delightful Christmas present to put in The Westgate's stocking.

*

The Westgate before Harold and Maude

The Twelve Chairs

THE TWELVE CHAIRS OPENED on Christmas Day, 1970, at both The Westgate and The Varsity theaters. Accompanying the film was a short animation, taken from the *2000-Year-Old Man* comedy routines created by Mel Brooks and Carl Reiner.

Written and directed by Mel Brooks, *The Twelve Chairs* is about a former aristocrat (Ron Moody) and a conman (Frank Langella), searching for hidden family jewels concealed in one of twelve chairs confiscated during the Soviet Revolution. Their chaotic treasure hunt pits them against a scheming priest (Dom DeLuise) as they race against each other to find the jewel-filled chair.

The Westgate's assistant manager William (Randy) Greene remembered the film: "It was an overlooked Mel Brooks movie and it kind of bombed when it came out. And so, they threw it in The Westgate and it played for twelve weeks, which was unheard of, because Westgate was one week or two at the most."

That was true. The last movie to run more than five weeks at The Westgate had been *How To Murder a Rich Uncle*, way back in 1958.

Its success at The Westgate was a little surprising. Upon its initial first-run release, *The Twelve Chairs* had gotten so-so to middling reviews.

Vincent Canby in *The New York Times* had this to say: "*The Twelve Chairs* is a

As they often did over the years, films would start at both The Westgate (the arty theater) and The Varsity (the college theater).

The Westgate before Harold and Maude

Ron Moody (left) and Frank Langella, the nobleman and the peasant, must work together to find the one chair from the set of twelve which contains the jewels.

comedy for Brooks watchers somewhat more indulgent than I. This is, I think, because Mr. Brooks' sense of humor is expressed almost entirely in varying degrees of rudeness and cruelty, unrelieved by any comic vision of mankind, of the Soviet Union, or even of his characters. In *The Twelve Chairs* Mr. Brooks wants to be lovable, and to stomp on your foot at the same time. I, for one, object."

Roger Ebert, in *The Chicago Sun-Times*, saw more in the movie than Canby. "*The Twelve Chairs* is the sort of movie that improves upon reflection," Ebert wrote. "You go in expecting to laugh a lot, because you've seen *The Producers*. And you do laugh a lot – to the point, perhaps, that you miss what this new Brooks film is about. It's not going for the laughs alone. It has something to say about honor among thieves, and by the end of the film we can sense a bond between the two main characters that is even, amazingly, human."

At its core, like the best Mel Brooks films (*The Producers, Young Frankenstein, Blazing Saddles*), it's ultimately a love story between two men. And, in the case of *The Twelve Chairs*, it also contains one of Brooks' best songs (*Hope For the Best / Expect the Worst*).

Local critic Don Morrison, writing in *The Minneapolis Star*, was an immediate fan of the film, saying it is "as preposterous and as much fun as a Roadrunner cartoon. It could go bad time and again, but it doesn't."

Morrison went on to write: "Brooks (who plays a drunken servant in the show) may be a reckless comic writer, yet he sort of tramples comic risks underfoot and wins every time. The whole thing is multiplied silliness, but I had the time of my life giggling at it. I might mention that I took a gang of boys, 10 to 14, to see the show. They laughed all the way home."

And later, once the film had settled in at The Westgate, *Minneapolis Tribune* columnist Will Jones stopped in to see what all the fuss was about.

"Mel Brooks has provided The Westgate Theater with one of those long-running, won't-quit hits," Jones observed. "Brooks' *The Twelve Chairs* has been running for a large handful of weeks, and even in the weekend's subzero weather was still causing parking jams in adjacent lots and streets.

"It is a far better piece of work than his first film *The Producers*, so that it would seem that he has learned something about moviemaking and learned fast. If the picture stays around long enough, I might be tempted to go back and have another look. The same response from earlier viewers may be helping to keep *The Twelve Chairs* around this long."

After *The Twelve Chairs* closed, Westgate regulars didn't have to wait long for another enduring hit. It was a matter of just a couple weeks before a film would come along to challenge (and then break) Mel Brooks' new record at the theater.

And ironically, it was a film by his old pal (and *2000-Year-Old Man* compatriot), Carl Reiner.

At 12 weeks, The Twelve Chairs was the longest-running movie in The Westgate's history ... up to that point.

The Westgate before Harold and Maude

Where's Poppa?

WHERE'S POPPA? (WRITTEN BY Robert Klane and directed by Carl Reiner) opened at The World Theater in downtown Minneapolis on Dec. 30, 1970.

A mere eleven days later, *Star Tribune* film critic Ben Kern wrote a review that was also something of a eulogy, lamenting the film's surprisingly sudden disappearance from local movie houses.

"The first film to be dropped from the bunch of goodies to hit town for the holiday season is *Where's Poppa?*," Kern wrote. "Dropped from The World, perhaps to return in the unpredictable future, perhaps not.

"It didn't catch on too well, one reason perhaps being that viewers hesitated to recommend it, lest they be considered tasteless at best, or some kind of perverts. Indeed, the first prerequisite for enjoying it lies in one's ability to build up a fast tolerance for those few verbal obscenities which until now have been considered too rotten for today's average libertine audience. Funny show, if you can stand the language."

Kern wasn't wrong. The language in the film was strong, even giving *Blazing Saddles* (which would be released four years later) a run for its money.

Where's Poppa? is a dark comedy about Gordon Hocheiser (George Segal), a lawyer who lives with his senile mother (Ruth Gordon), who constantly disrupts his life and romantic relationships. When Gordon falls for a beautiful nurse named Louise (Trish Van Devere), he becomes increasingly desperate to find a solution to his mother problem, leading to outrageous and politically incorrect attempts to place her elsewhere.

Roger Ebert, writing in *The Chicago

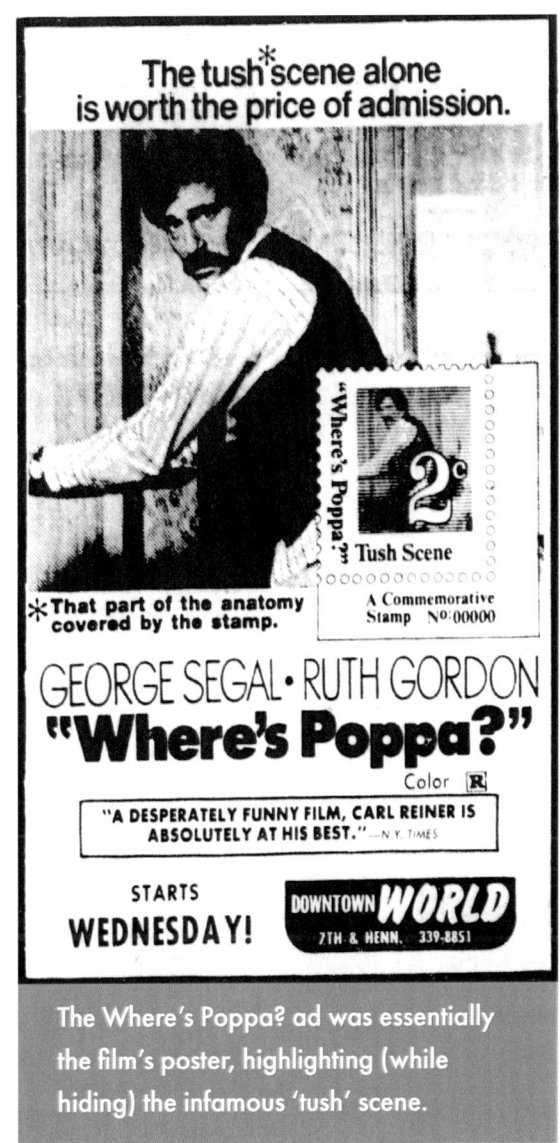

The Where's Poppa? ad was essentially the film's poster, highlighting (while hiding) the infamous 'tush' scene.

Sun-Times*, went so far as to explicitly warn his audience about … well … the explicitness.

"About a month after *The Producers* opened," Ebert wrote, "I got an indignant call from a lady who said she, for one, didn't see anything funny about a musical about Hitler. 'If you ask me,' she said, 'a musical like that should flop.' If you are that lady, don't go to see Carl Reiner's *Where's Poppa?* There is a certain kind of humor that rises below vulgarity. It isn't merely in the worst possible taste; it aspires to be in the worst possible taste."

And Vincent Canby seemed to agree, noting in his *New York Times* review, "Because it looks a lot more cruel than it really is, and because it sounds epically vulgar (the language is often deep blue), I was not at all surprised to read that at a recent convention of movie exhibitors in Bal Harbour, Florida, approximately 20 per cent of the audience walked out on the film, expressing their dismay, disgust and anger. I'd expect the same kind of reaction from a convention of madams at a hygiene movie."

The Twelve Chairs closed at The Westgate on May 5th, after a record-setting twelve week run. Three weeks later, *Where's Poppa?* opened at the theater.

Assistant manager Randy Greene explained that the reaction to this new film was similar to what had happened with *The Twelve Chairs*, which "played horribly when it first opened up. They put *Where's Poppa?* in The Westgate and it played for 36 weeks. It was a cult thing, people coming back again and again to see it."

Local writer Andy Sturdevant agreed. "I think they correctly sussed out that there was an appetite for less mainstream offerings," he said. "You could go to The Edina and see *The Poseidon Adventure*, or whatever, you know, dumb, big blockbuster. Or you'd go to The Westgate, and you could see something that was smaller scale and kind of weird. And you probably knew that there would be a bunch of other weirdos there, too."

Minneapolis Tribune columnist Will Jones was late to the party but quickly became a convert.

"*Where's Poppa?* keeps staying on and on at The Westgate theater, and I'm grateful," Jones wrote. "I missed its original opening and its revival opening and managed to see it only this week. It would have been a shame to miss such an experience. Experience? Well, the last time I can remember being so much at the mercy of a movie – that is, reduced to gasping, helpless laughter – was at the first of Peter Seller's Inspector Clouseau adventures.

"Carl Reiner has put together this fantastic down-home freak show, complete with

When it hit 24 weeks, Where's Poppa? had been at The Westgate for twice as long as The Twelve Chairs ... which had been there for twice as long as How To Murder a Rich Uncle.

The Westgate before Harold and Maude

characters running around in gorilla suits, in a manner to make Portnoy's complaint seem like a hangnail in comparison.

"The print at the Westgate is showing a little wear, but judging from the response of a midweek audience, the theater may be able to run the thing until the scratches obliterate Reiner's madness."

How to Murder a Rich Uncle had run for six weeks; *The Twelve Chairs* ran for twice that long. Carl Reiner then beat out his old pal Mel Brooks when Reiner's *Where's Poppa?* ran for nearly three times that of Brooks' *The Twelve Chairs*.

The folks at General Cinema might have been thinking, "Is it possible to find another movie that can match *Where's Poppa?* and its thirty-six week run?"

Perhaps. But they certainly weren't thinking there was a movie which could beat that record by three times.

General Cinema – and audiences – were about to be pleasantly surprised by an odd little movie called *Harold and Maude*.

Ruth Gordon and George Segal as a crazed mother and her exasperated son in Where's Poppa? Pauline Kael called Gordon's character "a senile psychopath."

George Segal, Ruth Gordon and Ron Liebman in a scene from Where's Poppa? Robert Klane's dark screenplay is not as dark as his novel, which adds incest to the other laundry list of taboo subjects in the movie.

HAROLD and MAUDE before the WESTGATE

The SCREENWRITER

THE STORY OF THE writing and sale of the *Harold and Maude* screenplay sounds like the most fanciful of Hollywood dreams: A young film student gets a job as the pool cleaner for a Hollywood producer; shows his work-in-progress to the producer's wife; she shows it to her husband; he promptly sells it to a major studio. And the movie gets made. Fade Out.

While all this is true, in the case of Colin Higgins and his screenplay for *Harold and Maude*, the complete story is even more fascinating. It all began with a notice on the bulletin board at UCLA, placed by Mildred Lewis, about the guest house behind her Bel Air mansion.

"'In exchange for light chauffeuring duties, pool cleaning duties and tennis court sweeping duties,'" Colin Higgins remembered the ad saying, "'there is a small place in the back of this Bel-Air mansion.' So, I put on a tie, went down there, interviewed with the lady of the house and got the place in the back for as long as I was at UCLA."

"Colin gave me the impression of being a very reliable and serious person," Mildred Lewis recalled, "and that is really what I wanted. I just liked him. He impressed me."

At the time, Higgins was working on the script that would become his short film thesis project. The idea for the film came from a strange inspiration: when he saw that he could rent a professional camera dolly for fifty dollars a day.

"You could raise the camera head to nine feet and drop it down to nine inches off the floor," he recalled. "So, I thought I would design a shot that would utilize that dolly to such an effect it would be well worth it.

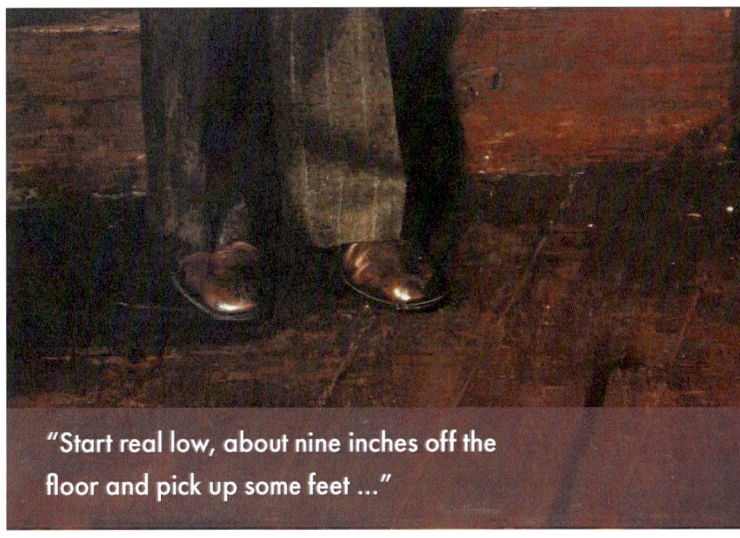
"Start real low, about nine inches off the floor and pick up some feet ..."

"...you'd follow the feet ..."

"... then you could move the dolly up a little further ..."

"... and you come around and you see him and he's hanging there ..."

"... then, someone should enter ..."

"... and what if she says, 'I suppose you think this is very funny, Harold' ..."

Harold and Maude before the Westgate

"And I thought, well, start real low, about nine inches off the floor, be moving around and pick up some feet, because that's what's down there. You'd follow the feet, and they would then stand up on a chair. And then you could move the dolly up a little further. And then the feet would kick over the chair and dangle in space. And I thought, 'wow, that's a great opening. You know, you've got the audience right away.'

"And then I thought, 'wait a minute. I mean, I've still got nine feet, I could go up nine feet.' And you come around and you see him and he's hanging there.

"Then, someone should enter. If you let a woman enter, you'll be able to hear her footsteps better. And you can hear footsteps off, and the woman arrives, and she screams. And I thought, what if she doesn't scream?

"So, she doesn't scream right away, she doesn't see him. She walks over to the desk and she's taking off her gloves. And what if she says, 'I suppose you think this is very funny, Harold.' And that's the cut."

With that sequence in mind, Higgins set about figuring out the rest of the plot threads which would grow into *Harold and Maude*.

Mildred Lewis' daughter, Susan, remembers Higgins recounting the story he was creating while he chauffeured her to and from school. "And at some point, I came home, and I told my mom about it," Susan Lewis recalled. "Because it was just amazing, just a great story. And my mom said, 'That sounds really interesting. I'd like to take a look at that.'"

As the wife of a successful film producer (Edward Lewis had produced *Spartacus*, *Seven Days in May* and *Grand Prix*, among many other films), Mildred was well-versed in reading screenplays.

"Ed was constantly pushing scripts at me, and truthfully, they were mostly very boring," she recalled. This was not the case with Colin's script. "I was sitting reading the script, and I found myself laughing out loud, and I thought, 'My God, this can't possibly be used for a class thesis; it's much too good.' And from there, I told Ed about it and put him to work at what he does best – promoting."

"I took it to Bob Evans and Peter Bart at Paramount," Edward Lewis explained. "One stop, that's all it took – left it with a kind of a deadline: this is a hot script, read it overnight and say yes or no."

The lightning speed of the process was not something Colin Higgins had anticipated.

"... and that's the cut."

"I'll never forget – I was sitting in the living room," Higgins recalled. "And Eddie (Lewis)

Edward and (Harold and Maude Executive Producer) Mildred Lewis

47

The entire opening sequence from Higgins' original thesis script was shot – nearly as written – by Hal Ashby as the first scene of the finished film.

was talking to Bob Evans, who was the head of Paramount at the time. And Eddie's saying, 'Well, you've got to make up your mind now Bob, otherwise we're gonna have to take it to Warner's.' Evans was saying, 'Well, can't you give us just another day?' And Eddie is saying, 'No, no, sorry, I can't.'"

This moxie amazed Colin Higgins. "And I'm thinking, 'Give him another day. Give him another day.' But he bought it."

Harold and Maude before the Westgate

The DIRECTOR

THE ORIGINAL PLAN – at least in Colin's mind – was that he would both write and direct the film.

"The script was sold with me as the director," Higgins explained. "Because I was still in that film school mode, where you don't sell anything unless you get to direct it. Paramount said, 'You should do a Director's Test first,' that was part of the agreement. They would give me about $7,000 and I would show them that I could direct.

"So, I made the test, with a different cast but with a professional group of people. We shot it on the stages at Columbia for two days: three scenes, $7,500. They saw the test and they decided that they would prefer another director. They were unimpressed, and in fact, I think, had no intention of letting me direct the movie at all."

Paramount production executive Peter Bart had his own thoughts on the perfect director for this unique project: Hal Ashby, who at that point had only one feature to his name as a director: *The Landlord*.

"I remember realizing what an amazingly original voice the *(Harold and Maude)* script represented," Bart recalled, "provided that you could find the filmmaker who would get it. I had seen *The Landlord*, and (that film's producer) Norman Jewison was a friend of mine. He too was very high on Hal."

However, one key person disagreed with Peter Bart. And that was Hal Ashby.

Ashby had entered the business as an editor and had worked successfully with producer/director Norman Jewison, winning an

Hal Ashby (on the left, with the beard), watching white-suited Beau Bridges in Ashby's first feature film, The Landlord.

Academy Award for editing *In the Heat of the Night*. Ashby had directed his first feature and was looking for his next project. But he wasn't one to be rushed into anything.

Ashby's producing partner, Charles Mulvehill, remembered: "Early on, Hal was very, very picky about the projects that he chose. I mean, he went through tons of scripts before he found *Harold and Maude*."

Ashby read the script, liked it, but then learned that its screenwriter wanted to direct the film. And had even shot a test.

"I went back to Paramount," Ashby remembered. "And I said, 'Why the hell don't you just let Colin make his film? He sees it and he wants to make it.' They said, 'No. If you don't do it, we're going to get somebody else anyway.'"

So, Ashby sat down with Higgins and had a conversation. "I talked to Colin about it, and he said yes, he would feel good about my doing it," Ashby recalled. "I said, 'O.K.'"

Harold and Maude had its director. Now they just needed some actors to direct.

Ruth Gordon had recently won an Academy Award for *Rosemary's Baby* – which was why, at the time, "Everyone wants Ruth Gordon."

Harold and Maude before the Westgate

CASTING

Colin Higgins, now a co-producer on the film, entered the casting phase with some very definite ideas. He had written the two leads with specific actors in mind: his friend, actor John Rubinstein as Harold, and Elsa Lanchester (perhaps best known for her roles in *The Bride of Frankenstein*) as Maude.

"That's who he always envisioned in that part," John Rubinstein remembered. "And if you read Maude's lines with Elsa Lanchester in mind, you'll see how well it fits."

However, Hal Ashby had other ideas.

"There were two women in contention for the Maude role," producer Charles Mulvehill remembered. "Dame Edith Evans, she was a very good actress, and very serious. And then there was Ruth (Gordon). And it was a big quandary for Hal, which way to go, because obviously each actress brought their own kind of persona to the piece."

"When I read *Harold and Maude*, I thought that part's meant for me. I think I am Maude," Ruth Gordon recalled. "The director invited me to come over. He talked, I talked, we talked.

"'Well,' I said, 'do you want me?' 'Oh,' he said, 'everybody wants Ruth Gordon. But I'm flying to London tonight to interview some English actresses.'

"Well, the hell with him, I thought."

Ashby did fly to London to meet with Edith Evans (among other actresses), but purportedly she laughed at the description of Maude in the script and said, "That doesn't sound like me, ducky. Why don't you get Ruth Gordon?"

So, Hal Ashby had his Maude.

But that London casting trip was not for naught: it provided him with the perfect actress to play Harold's mother – Vivian Pickles.

The Harold and Maude cast that might have been: John Rubinstein and Elsa Lanchester.

"I have John Schlesinger to thank for my role in *Harold and Maude*," Vivian Pickles explained. "I'd been in *Sunday Bloody Sunday* for John. He had given Hal Ashby my name to look up when Hal was interviewing all the famous English dames in a penthouse suite at the top of London's Dorchester Hotel.

"The script was gorgeous to read. It just came right off the page. And we chatted and he just beamed. He then altered (the roles). We got the English person for the American woman, and he used the American woman for what was going to be an English bawdy Dame, which was Ruth Gordon. So poor old darling English Dames didn't get any work, but I was very grateful!"

The casting process also proved to be serendipitous for producer Charles Mulvehill.

"Computer date number two, Edith Fern," Mulvehill recalled, "was described in the script as kind of a female Don Knotts. It was really difficult trying to find that person who fit that description.

"(Shari Summer's) manager had taken her to William Morris to meet some agents, and that's when (legendary casting director) Lynn

Vivian Pickles (with Bernard Holley) in *Elizabeth R.*, which aired on BBC2 in the UK and on PBS Masterpiece Theater in the U.S.

Stalmaster saw her. I remember him calling me saying he found her. And he was really excited, because that was a hard role to cast.

"And it was all her own wardrobe – that's how much she fit into that character," Mulvehill continued. "At any rate we met, and during the postproduction period, we got married, and we still are married. It's been an interesting trip."

But one casting hurdle remained: Who was going to play the co-title role of Harold Parker Chasen?

"We tested a lot of people for Harold," producer Mulvehill recalled. "I mean, trying to figure out who was the right combination of weird little kid that would make this work?"

"It's sort of well-known that Bud was not my first choice for *Harold and Maude*," Colin Higgins confirmed. "We did a test of about six different people for Harold, and Bud was my second choice. My first choice was an actor I had gone to UCLA with, Johnny Rubinstein."

"Colin and I met and knew each other at UCLA, in the Theater Arts Department, which we both attended between 1964 and 1968," Rubinstein told me. "Colin was a graduate student, working on his Master's. He was also a wonderful actor and did a stunning job in the Department's production of *The Importance of Being Earnest*. Colin knew that I would interpret the words and try to make them fly and make them real."

After the screen test, Colin Higgins concurred. "Johnny had done it absolutely the way that I had written it."

But Ashby wasn't sold. "I wanted an actor who, of course, looked young enough," Ashby explained. "That was much more difficult – although all casting's difficult – than the casting for Ruth's part. I must have met fifty boys from different places, and I finally ended up testing six."

"All the tests were shot at Hal Ashby's house," Ruth Gordon recalled. "Bob Balaban was the first to test. Darling Bob Balaban didn't get the job. Did he look too good-natured, too young?"

Four other actors, including John Rubinstein, screen-tested for the role. But everyone – including Bud Cort – agreed that Cort was perfect for the part.

Harold and Maude before the Westgate

"I walked into this room and Hal [Ashby] was the first person I saw," Bud Cort remembered. "Hal made me feel so warm and welcome. He said, 'This is Colin Higgins who wrote the script, this is Chuck Mulvehill who's producing it.' And I just looked at all three of them and said, 'I'm playing this part.' And Hal laughed and said, 'I guess you are!'"

Even competitor John Rubinstein (who went on to create the title role in Bob Fosse's legendary stage musical, *Pippin*) ultimately agreed with the choice.

"I was very disappointed, not getting *Harold and Maude*. But I absolutely *loved* the finished version of *Harold and Maude*. And I immediately saw that Bud Cort was nothing short of perfect to play that complicated role. He captured Colin's dark and silly and ultimately moving character beautifully."

Colin Higgins concurred: "I think Hal made the right choice. I think Bud goes beyond playing the part and becomes the part."

Shari Summers as Computer Date #2, Edith Fern.

"I'm playing this part."

PRODUCTION

Once casting was locked in, the next decision was where to shoot the film. For Ashby, the decision was an easy one: As far from the Hollywood suits as he could get.

"He didn't talk to them from the day we started shooting," producer Mulvehill remembered. "His attitude was, and this would not fly at all today, but his attitude was, 'Look, studio – you've made a decision, and you want me to direct this movie. You've made that decision. Now beat it. We've talked about what it's going to cost and what the schedule is and we've all agreed to that. And now leave me the fuck alone, because I'm making this movie. That's what you've hired me to do.'"

The San Francisco area offered the right look for the exteriors and the proper distance from the studio in Los Angeles. Then it came down to finding the specific locations.

"All the interiors and exteriors of the mansion were set up in a place called the Cameron Estate, which is in Hillsboro, about thirty

The Cameron Estate – the perfect location for the interiors and the exteriors.

Hal Ashby and Vivian Pickles chat while heading down toward the pool at The Cameron Estate.

Bud Cort, Vivian Pickles and Ellen Geer shooting inside the Cameron Estate.

Harold and Maude before the Westgate

miles from San Francisco," Mulvehill remembered. "We had a very difficult time securing this location because there had been an Otto Preminger film that had shot in Hillsboro years before. That production was pretty outrageous, and they created all kinds of problems. So, securing this location required a lot of negotiations."

Actress Vivian Pickles thought the location was "a marvelous place. We only had it for a week. And we had to work very hard to finish everything in that week. And we did get it done," she explained, because "Hal's editor side gave his director side a shortcut," so that he wasn't shooting things he wouldn't use in the finished film.

Ellen Geer, who played the third computer date (Sunshine Doré), concurred: "It was this wonderful old mansion that was empty," she recalled, "but was taken care of by a very sweet couple. It was a wonderful location."

The other tricky location was figuring out where Maude lived. In the screenplay, it's called out as simply "Maude's Apartment," with the following description:

INT. MAUDE'S APARTMENT — DAY

We see Maude's main room filled with all kinds of eccentric memorabilia, from a mounted swordfish to an ivory Buddha. It is dominated by a large, canopied bed like something from a Wagnerian opera. Other features are a large fireplace, a baby grand piano, expensive paintings on the walls, a tall wooden sculpture, and a Japanese type eating area with satin cushions.

"We were meeting Art Directors, and the first question out of our mouths was, 'What does Maude live in? What do you see?,'" producer Mulvehill remembered. "And the obvious

"This is all memorabilia... but it's incidental, not integral, if you know what I mean."

Maude's train car home is still available for tours to this day at the Western Railway Museum in Solano County, California.

answer is an apartment or a little flat or whatever. And (Production Designer) Michael Haller came in and he brought his own kind of special 'bent' to the piece. He brought the railroad car."

Camera Operator Joe Marquette was not only impressed with that location, but also at the level of detail the Art Department provided.

"The thing about the railroad car," he said, "if you opened up the drawers of (Maude's) sewing machine area, all the thimbles and threads would be in there, all the needles. If you went over to her desk and opened up a drawer, there would be all these postcards written out with letters. Every single drawer had stuff from Maude's life. That's the level of detail that Mike (Haller) asked his assistant to go to."

But while the train car location was a hit, the decision of where to locate it – near the airport – turned out to have more downsides than upsides.

"We had the great idea of parking it on a siding that was right near the airport," Mulvehill recalled. "Because we thought, well, we'll be able to get our dailies back and forth to be processed and won't that be great? Not thinking that near the airport we had to deal with the noise of the aircraft taking off. So that was a learning experience for us."

Once they got down to the actual shooting, the mood that Ashby created on the set was conducive to getting the best out of people and allowing them to bring their ideas to the table.

"Most (directors) at that time, they would say, 'Lights, Camera, Action!' or something like that," actress Judy Engles (computer date Candy Gulf) remembered.

But that wasn't the case with Hal Ashby.

"I can still remember this, I can hear him go, 'Lights, Camera, (softly) Judy,'" Engels recalled with a laugh. "And he wouldn't even say it like there was a big, exciting thing about to happen. I remember his voice being really sweet, and calming, and soothing. I never worked with anybody who didn't say, 'Action!' where they didn't get crazy instead of

Some final touch-ups for Judy Engels.

Bud Cort: "He took a chance on me and in so doing became not only a director, but a father, a mother, a driving instructor, and a psychiatric nurse."

The costume designer's brilliant idea: matching outfits for psychiatrist and patient. "We looked for ways to amuse ourselves."

calm. I remember that about Hal. I remember the whole thing being very easy."

Bud Cort agreed. "I was an emotional minefield," Cort recalled. "He took a chance on me and in so doing became not only a director, but a father, a mother, a driving instructor, and a psychiatric nurse. It was a difficult part for me, but Hal was so sympathetic, so understanding. And I think back on it now, I must have driven him crazy, but he never ever complained, and he was there twenty-four hours a day, six days a week."

Actress Vivian Pickles shared that sentiment. "Hal was so inspiring, with a most wonderful, genuine, appreciative smile of warm approval that spurred you on," she said. "He really loved my ideas – particularly for my favorite scene, where Mrs. Chasen fills out the application form for her son's dating service."

But Ashby understood that good ideas could come from anywhere.

"Bill Theiss, our costume designer, came up with this idea," Mulvehill recalled. "Every time Harold met with his psychiatrist, he was

Harold and Maude before the Westgate

Hal and Ruth chatting, perhaps about on-set safety.

dressed exactly as a psychiatrist. It was just a little funny bit that may be missed, but we looked for ways to amuse ourselves."

For Bud Cort, that openness to ideas produced some classic moments in the film.

"I remember once, it was just a gorgeous sunset, and we had done some shots," Cort recalled. "And I said to Hal, 'What about if I picked her up and gave her a piggyback?' He said that would be fabulous. So, I went up to Ruth, and she said, 'What did you have in mind?' 'Well, I thought maybe if I gave you a piggyback ride?'

"And she said, 'That's a great idea. Where's the stunt girl?' Two seconds later, the girl had the coat on, and I did it with the stunt girl.

"Ruth was very careful. When she would walk on a set, the first thing she would do was look around and see where the cables were. She was not going to break her neck on the set at her age. She was just careful that way."

While Ruth Gordon avoided any physical mishaps, the production was blessed (and cursed) with some memorable moments.

Hal Ashby and Ellen Geer discuss Harakiri as Bud Cort looks on.

Harold and Maude before the Westgate

HAPPY (and NOT SO HAPPY) ACCIDENTS

When it came to actual, physical accidents, Stunt Coordinator Buddy Joe Hooker recalled that there "was only one dark spot in the movie."

"It was the scene where the El Camino goes by and the motorcycle cop runs and gets on his bike and chases after them," Hooker recalled. "The guy playing the cop (William Lucking) had probably done it three or four times. And it was this long sweeping turn, and by the time he got to the end of the run he was probably in fourth gear doing sixty or something like that. And on about the fourth take, we see he didn't put the kickstand up."

While making the turn, Lucking was thrown off the bike and tossed down a sixty-foot embankment, landing in a two-foot mud puddle, which – to some extent – helped to break his fall.

"I've seen the piece of film," Lucking recalled. "It looked like a rag doll. I can recall it right up to the point where my leg got crushed. Some doctor came down when I was laying in the mud and he gave me a shot of some kind and said, 'Don't worry, you'll feel better after this.' He left and they took me to the hospital. I don't remember a whole lot after that."

"Luckily he wasn't seriously hurt," Mulvehill explained. "But it was bad enough that he couldn't do the role. So that's when I asked Tom Skerritt, a friend of ours, if he'd do it as a cameo."

"One of the funniest things that ever happened on that film," Hal Ashby recounted, "was when I got Tom Skerritt as the motorcycle cop. Tom is a very loose actor, but whatever he would say, Ruth would still say her lines. She was a stage actor and those were her lines, and if those were the lines, that's where she was going."

When it came to billing, Skerritt offered an odd option.

As Skerritt explained, "It was sort of last

Bud Cort, Ruth Gordon and the replacement motorcycle cop, Tom Skerritt.

Hal Ashby with the Motorcycle Officer, played by M. Borman (aka Tom Skerritt)

minute. Chuck Mulvehill, Hal and I were having a few beers and Chuck said, 'What about billing on this?' And I said, 'How about this: Whatever happened to Martin Bormann? He was second in command to Adolf Hitler. No one knows what happened to Martin Bormann.' And I said, 'Martin Bormann went to Oakland, California and became a motorcycle cop.'"

And so that character is listed in the credits as simply: M. Borman.

Throughout the production, Ashby was always open to ideas and taking advantage of unplanned moments. As Mulvehill recalled, "One of Hal's strong suits was to be able to get involved with people and to explore all of these ideas. Nothing was put down in terms of an idea."

"(Production Designer) Michael Haller's father had just passed away," Mulvehill continued. "And at his funeral, there was a band – a marching band – that happened to be going down the street. And Michael thought that would be kind of an incongruous image, both visually and sound-wise, for this funeral. So, we threw that in."

Steven Spielberg: "That's one of the most famous shots in the world."

Harold and Maude before the Westgate

The very frustrating (some say cheesy) freeze frame.

For Ellen Geer, the bit that Ashby threw in was when she slipped while making an exit in one scene. "I slipped on this marble floor," Geer recalled. "And I just kept going – because you know, as a theatre-trained actor, you don't stop for that and say, 'Cut' – you just keep going. And he loved it! In fact, I heard him snicker. So, we just kept going. He was wonderful to work with."

One of the film's most iconic moments also grew out of Ashby's willingness to try something different and let the actors follow their instincts.

"Like when we did the scene with Vivian Pickles and Judy Engles (Candy Gulf)," Bud Cort recalled. "Where Judy runs out of the room screaming, and I looked at Vivian and I looked back. And I knew Hal would never cut until we were finished with that, and I was still acting.

"So, I just slowly turned toward the camera, and I mean, Steven Spielberg said that's one of the most famous shots in the world. And that's because we were all living that film moment to moment."

That shot – The Look, as it's come to be known – is still remembered today. As filmmaker Edgar Wright explained, "In the canon of great looks to camera, breaking the fourth wall, I think *Harold and Maude* has one of the all timers. It's just perfect."

One other iconic moment which wasn't planned is the freeze frame as Harold's car goes over the cliff. It wasn't supposed to happen that way. In fact, they were prepared to capture the moment from a number of different angles.

"We had like five cameras," Mulvehill recalled. "Of course, the camera that was in the car got destroyed in the crash. The slow-motion camera broke down. So, we ended up with not very many angles of this moment, which just drove Hal to distraction, because there was no way it could be fixed. And it was not one that we could go back and re shoot.

"So, we have this cheesy stop frame in the middle of the car going over the cliff. And it always bugged Hal. It bugged all of us, but what are you going to do?"

65

Bud Cort, Hal Ashby and Ruth Gordon discuss the tree which Maude will re-plant in a somewhat truncated scene later.

POST-PRODUCTION

With shooting behind them, Ashby and his team had to deal with the hours and hours (and hours) of footage they'd shot.

"Hal shot a lot of film," producer Mulvehill explained. "Not necessarily a lot of takes, but he shot lots of coverage, lots of different angles. He loved to have… he just wanted someplace to go."

Ashby agreed. "I have a tendency, when shooting a film, I would rather not limit myself – except for rare instances when I visually lock into a thing and say, 'That would be a sensational transition.' I'll still probably cover myself, so I'll have two or three different openings and ways to get in and out of the scene and make those transitions work."

After weeks of editing, the first cut ran long.

"The first assembly of the film was three hours long," Mulvehill recalled. "I remember looking at it and thinking that my career had begun and ended, because it was just awful. It was long and tedious. You wanted to strangle Maude. If she opened up and laid out one more pontification, you just wanted to slug her. It was just awful."

"The script was overwritten," Ashby explained. "In the sense that scenes had a tendency to go on and on, becoming much more philosophical than they should. Like you'd get into a scene that would go on for three or four minutes, expounding this philosophy – well you'd say, 'My God if you don't quit saying it, I'm going to get bored with it.'"

For example, here's one 'Maude philosophy' scene as written:

EXT. A PLEASANT GLADE IN THE FOREST – DAY

Maude and Harold have just finished planting the tree;
Maude is putting the finishing touches around the trunk.
She stands up.

MAUDE
There. Oh, I like the feel of soil, don't you? And the smell. It's the earth. "The earth is my body. My head is in the stars."
(little laugh)
Who said that?

HAROLD
I don't know.

MAUDE
I suppose I did.
(laughs)
Well, farewell little tree. Grow up tall, and change, and fall to replenish the earth. Isn't it wonderful, Harold? All around us. Living things.

EXT. THE FOREST – DAY

Harold and Maude are sitting in a tree.

MAUDE
I come here as often as I can. It's exhilarating. What do you call it? Nature! Life! Soul! God! At any rate, it's here, and…

We PULL BACK on the ZOOM and see they are sitting in the top branches of a very tall tree.

MAUDE
... we are part of it.

And here's what ended up in Ashby's final cut:

EXT. A PLEASANT GLADE IN THE FOREST – DAY

Maude and Harold have just finished planting the tree;
Maude is putting the finishing touches around the trunk.
She stands up.

MAUDE
There. Oh, I love the feel of soil, don't you? And the smell. It's the earth. "The earth is my body. My head is in the stars."
(little laugh)
Who said that?

HAROLD
I don't know.

MAUDE
I suppose I did.
(laughs)
Isn't it wonderful, Harold? All around us.
Living things.

"We took an hour and a half out of the film and did not lose one scene," Mulvehill explained. "There was just that much superfluous dialogue in the movie, as it turns out. And a lot of these scenes were cut in half, basically. But the essence of the scene still came through, and I guess, in the end, that's all that's important."

A scene lost in the trimming process: Maude in the church, preparing to "paint the saint."

Harold and Maude before the Westgate

Peter Bart's two "disreputable" visitors: Hal Ashby and Cat Stevens (Yusuf Islam).

The MUSIC

Hal Ashby started thinking about the music for the film from the very beginning – in fact, right after being hired for the job.

"Hal loved the script but couldn't figure out his perspective on it," recalled Paramount production executive Peter Bart. "He was searching for a point of view. Then one day he called me to say, 'I want to bring over a friend.' He appeared with Cat (Stevens), whose album was just becoming hot.

"The two of them were bearded hippies who looked like they'd just got off a bus from Haight Ashbury. I considered bringing them in to meet (Robert) Evans, but in that period, Bob dressed like an impeccably groomed studio chief with dark grey suits and white shirts and black ties – I felt he would not 'get' his disreputable visitors."

This idea of working on the music even before shooting had begun wasn't a new idea for Ashby.

"The music plays a big part in any of my films," he explained. "I had it happen as an editor on *In the Heat of the Night*. I'd just gotten a Ray Charles album and was listening to it."

To keep from getting bored, Ashby would play the music while looking through silent footage. And the habit continued while editing *Harold and Maude*.

"What I always used to tell the guys – the editors who were working in L.A. when we were shooting up North," Ashby explained. "Anything we sent down that was silent, I said, just grab a track – any track of Cat's – and put it with it. So, if I'm watching dailies, and it's three or four minutes silent, at least it will be with music. It'll bring it to life, and I'll just get ideas from it."

While Hal was excited about the idea, Yusuf/Cat Stevens wasn't quite so sure.

"I was a little bit cautious," Yusuf remembered. "I said, 'Hang on, this is a comedy, and my music is quite serious. I take it quite

Harold and Maude before the Westgate

seriously.' So, he invited me to San Francisco where they were filming it and watching the rushes. And we were sitting there – and he was puffing on his little, whatever it was – and he was saying, 'Look at this.' And there was *Miles From Nowhere* and the hearse, and I went, 'Oh, that's good.'"

Ashby drew heavily from two of the existing albums (*Tea for the Tillerman* and *Mona Bone Jakon*), but also asked for two more songs: *Don't Be Shy* for the opening credits, and *If You Want To Sing Out Sing Out*, which Maude would perform and which would be used over the closing credits. So, Yusuf went ahead and wrote the songs and produced two demos for Ashby to use during editing.

"I always intended to do those songs properly," Yusuf explained. "But Hal stuck them in the film, because he probably had a deadline to get the film out. And I was a little bit horrified when I heard it. They were still demos to me.

"But the strange thing is everybody loves those songs because they're so raw and so natural, so free and with no self-consciousness about them. And that's what made the songs kind of perfect for the film."

Ultimately, Colin Higgins agreed.

"I never really got that (Cat) Stevens' contribution was as great as it is until I got to France," Higgins remembered. "And I saw *Harold and Maude* there in English, but with French subtitles. I was reading the subtitles, and they also subtitled the songs, so I would be reading the lyrics.

"It was amazing, because when I listen to his songs, they are so familiar that my ear doesn't pick up the lyrics. But when I saw the lyrics written down in front of me, I was amazed at how they complemented the film."

"At the end, more than half the audience got to its feet and applauded. I'd never seen that at a preview."

The PREVIEW

IT WAS NOW TIME to preview the movie in front of an audience.

Paramount executive Robert Evans was there. "We previewed in Palo Alto, near Stanford," he recalled. "I had envisioned the worst. I had previews in those days where there was no one in the theatre at the end of the picture. I'll never forget the preview. We got the best reaction of any feature we ever had."

His co-worker, Peter Bart agreed. "I sat there, watching the film for the first time with an audience, and I couldn't believe what I saw. The movie, with all of its odd moments and stray tunes, came together brilliantly. It was a completely realized piece of filmmaking.

"At the end, more than half the audience got to its feet and applauded. I'd never seen that at a preview. I literally shook with excitement, then hugged Hal, who was in shock. The kids in the audience followed us outside and wanted to talk about the movie. They wouldn't quit."

"This movie previewed great," Mulvehill agreed. "I remember somebody from the marketing department at Paramount came up and said that it had previewed better than any movie since Jerry Lewis, because I guess they previewed very, very well. Which led us to think that we were really going to have a successful film."

"I had two feelings leaving that screening," Peter Bart recalled. "One, the picture worked beautifully. Two, my company (Paramount) was ill-suited to sell it."

Bart was correct on both counts.

Harold and Maude before the Westgate

The MARKETING

The marketing campaign for *Harold and Maude* was so disastrous that even to this day filmmakers look back on it in awe.

"I love that the poster to *Harold and Maude* was just the words 'Harold and Maude,'" filmmaker Judd Apatow said. "They didn't even know how to put a picture on it. They're like, 'What can we do here?' I mean, you can imagine the marketing panic."

"If you've ever seen the original poster for *Harold and Maude*, you know that it's a disgrace," offered Colin Higgins. "It looked like it was done on a hand-press."

Regardless of the size or shape, the original movie poster (according to Colin Higgins) was "a disgrace."

The Kiss got axed from the movie, but you can still find it online in the original trailer.

Producer Mildred Lewis agreed: "I think they got some grade school student to do it for them."

Paramount executive Peter Bart put it most bluntly and succinctly: "We had the worst campaign in the history of American film."

"Nobody knew what to do or how to sell this movie," producer Mulvehill explained. "So, we talked Paramount into letting Pablo Ferro do a trailer. Pablo had done all these trailers for Stanley Kubrick. He was a really inventive, out of the box guy that really understood film and understood where Hal was."

"The trailer that I did, Bob Evans hated it," Pablo Ferro explained. "Because I used a shot of Bud Cort kissing Ruth Gordon. He didn't like that. I told him that I didn't see anything wrong with it and I asked him, 'Did you read the script?' Because it's a love story about an older person and a younger person. There's nothing bad about it."

"Pablo and I were kind of surprised that they were that angry about it," Mulvehill recalled. "I mean, they were angry about it. It was not the movie they were releasing, as far as they were concerned. And, I think, therein lies the problem."

"The advertising people at Paramount had no idea what to do with the movie," Peter Bart explained. "They opened it at Christmastime with a tombstone ad. Nobody came. The movie died. I was in shock. Here was a perfect oddball movie. The preview audience had loved it. How could it simply perish?"

Harold and Maude before the Westgate

The REVIEWS

"It opened and closed in a week," Mulvehill said. "You couldn't drag people in. We thought it was a great film. It was really a shock when it was released and nobody cared. Nobody came and nobody cared."

"We opened at the Village Theater in Westwood at Christmas," Colin Higgins remembered. "And the reason we had all these large, large theaters across the country was that *The Godfather* wasn't ready, and Paramount booked *The Godfather* into all these theaters for Christmas. These theaters had nothing to play. Paramount told them, 'We've got this little comedy called *Harold and Maude*,' and the theaters had no choice."

"I'll never forget, the first review was in *Variety*," Mulvehill recalled. "His opening line was '*Harold and Maude* is as funny as a burning orphanage.' And Peter Bart said *Time* magazine was going to do us a favor and not review the film. We were stunned. What can I say – we were stunned."

Many critics agreed with *Variety*. Roger Ebert opened his review with this: "Death can be as funny as most things in life, I suppose, but not the way *Harold and Maude* go about it."

However, a handful of critics praised the film, with Charles Champlin of *The Los Angeles Times* saying the film was "stylish, nutty, enjoyable and oddly provocative," while Pauline Kael thought it was "made with considerable wit and skill."

And Judith Crist offered up the blurb which would drive the film's marketing campaign from that point forward: "It's a joy. An enchanting excursion into the joy of living. Wonderfully perceptive satiric jabs at motherhood, the military, psychiatry and computer dating. Bud Cort is the very embodiment of boyhood. Ruth Gordon is beautifully restrained and deeply touching. Hers is a performance to cherish."

However, it was Vincent Canby's negative review in *The New York Times* that Ruth Gordon found particularly irksome. In it he wrote (among other things): "You might well want to miss Hal Ashby's *Harold and Maude*, a comedy that pretends to be as thoroughly in favor of life as *You Can't Take It With You*, whereas it's quite as much about death as it appears to be."

Paramount slipped Harold and Maude into the slot for the not-quite-ready The Godfather, with less than stellar results.

Gordon was so annoyed with his response to the movie she actually sat down and wrote the critic a letter.

Dear Mr. Canby,

What a disappointment to read your review. I know people aren't supposed to write a critic and the last time I did was fifty-six years ago today. I got a good review in the December 22, 1915 Times and wrote the critic. It was my first time on the stage, and I didn't know you shouldn't.

The Judith Crist rave/quote really drove the early advertising attempts.

Today I know, but I'm doing it. I wish you'd liked Harold and Maude. They said you saw it in a screening room with a dozen other critics. I wish you could have seen it with an audience. Maybe you wouldn't have liked it then, but then I'd feel you saw it the way it was meant

Harold and Maude before the Westgate

to be seen. Shoulder to shoulder with people is how a play or film is written to be seen, and I wish you'd seen it that way.

Forgive the letter. Maybe it's all right to do if you only do it every fifty-six years.

Ruth Gordon

The movie received a more favorable critical response when it opened at The World Theater in downtown Minneapolis at Christmastime, but it wasn't enough to draw the necessary crowds.

Critic Don Morrison at *The Minneapolis Star* wrote: "*Harold and Maude* is a glorious addition to a class of movies that I might as well admit I love simply because they are. *Harold and Maude* ranks up high with those delicious nut movies – quirky, off-beat, throwaway, preposterous. They aren't about any form of real life to be observed on this planet – which is part of their charm – but simply take a great loony idea and wing it as far as it will go."

Morrison's counterpart over at the *Minneapolis Tribune*, critic Ben Kern, agreed: "Ruth Gordon is on-the-button as Maude, the fey, intrepid open enemy of all standards but her own. And Bud Cort is equally convincing as Harold, the appealing, sensitive victim of family domination. Ironically enough, the people who feel revulsion at the age disparity (as does Harold's family cleric: 'Makes me want to vomit,' he says) stand to gain something by seeing the film."

Harold and Maude opened on Christmas Day, 1971, at The World Theater in downtown Minneapolis. Despite the strong reviews, *Harold and Maude* disappeared from The World (in more ways than one) in early January 1972.

Two months later, it would be back with a vengeance.

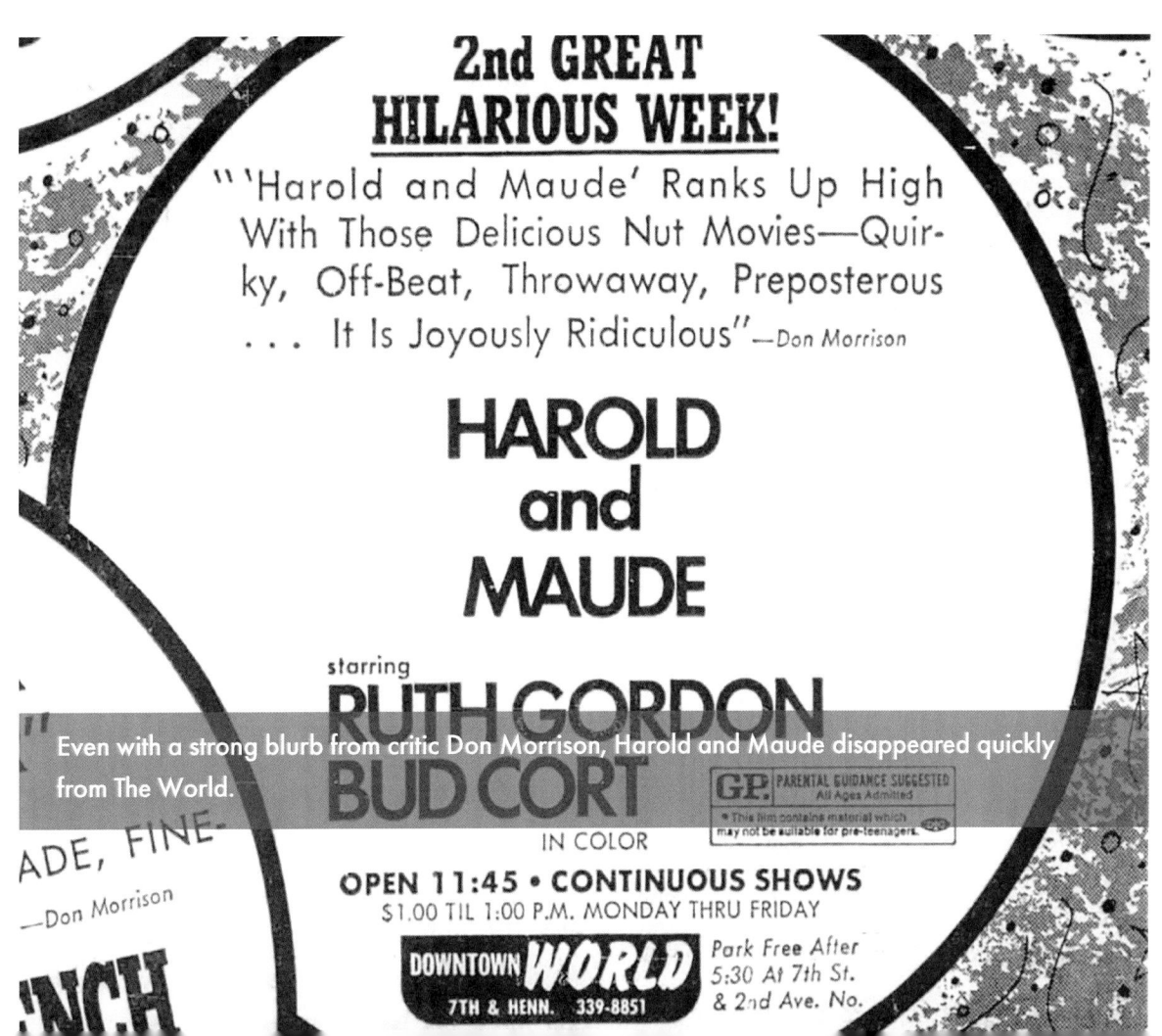

Even with a strong blurb from critic Don Morrison, Harold and Maude disappeared quickly from The World.

HAROLD AND
STARTING THIRD
SOME VARIETY
PLEASE
HAROLD & MAUDE
NEED
A CHANGE OF SCENE
ANOTHER OPENING
SHOW
NEIGHBORHOOD
WESTGATE
TWO YEARS
TOO MUCH
THE SHOW GO ON
ON AND ON

HAROLD and MAUDE at the WESTGATE

The RESURRECTION

AT THE SAME TIME that *Harold and Maude* was bombing in downtown Minneapolis, *Where's Poppa?* was wrapping up its remarkable thirty-six week run at The Westgate.

This was followed by the Australian film, *Walkabout*, and then by a Liza Minelli double-feature (*The Sterile Cuckoo* and *Charlie Bubbles*).

Recognizing that *Harold and Maude* had gotten pretty strong local reviews ... while also understanding that The Westgate was getting a reputation for resuscitating oddball comedies, such as *The Twelve Chairs* and *Where's Poppa?* ... someone at General Cinema decided that *Harold and Maude* might be a good fit at The Westgate Theater.

That was their first smart move. The second smart move was including the short that had run with it at The World Theater: *De Düva*.

When *Minneapolis Tribune* columnist Will Jones learned that this return of *Harold and Maude* would include the short *De Düva*, he was thrilled.

"A 15-minute movie that I've been hoping to see for a year or more is reopening in town this week," Jones wrote in his column on Monday, March 20. "And with a little luck, maybe it'll stay long enough to get the attention it deserves."

Jones then went on to wax ecstatic about the short, and the pleas he had made to General Cinema to bring the film back. Apparently, they heard him.

"Now they're bringing *Harold and Maude* back for a run at The Westgate Theater," Jones wrote, "which has become a sort of nursing

home for mistreated film comedies that don't have time to catch on with their true public in the frenzy of normal Downtown first runs and quickie neighborhood runs."

"And they're bringing back *De Düva* for additional support. Despite its short running time, the Bergman spoof qualifies as a second feature, and anyone venturing to The Westgate to see *Harold and Maude* starting Wednesday should certainly make a point of getting there in time to see the short subject."

Two days after the column came out, *Harold and Maude* (and the short, *De Düva*) opened at The Westgate Theater.

Assistant manager Randy Greene remembered what happened. "I was not there Wednesday," he told me. "Thursday, when I walked in, everyone said, 'This place was nuts last night.'

"And then of course it was nuts Thursday night as well. It was just nuts. People were just piling in. So that article jumpstarted the thing and basically it was word of mouth. It took off after that. But that Will Jones article really did make it start."

Harold and Maude at the Westgate

EVERYBODY'S TALKING ABOUT "HAROLD & MAUDE"

At Christmas time in 1970, "Where's Poppa?" got lost among the boxoffice bonanzas. At Christmas time in 1971, the same fate befell "Harold and Maude." Seen by few, but loved by all, it captured the hearts of the same group of comedy fans. At their urging, we are giving you another chance to see this hilarious comedy.

THE CRITICS ARE TALKING ABOUT "HAROLD & MAUDE"

"WILL JONES of the Minneapolis Tribune said "I was close to blacking out from the laughter . . . I haven't felt myself in such a state of peril for several years . . . sheer lunacy"

DON MORRISON of the Minneapolis Star in his review said " 'Harold and Maude' ranks up high with those delicious nut movies — quirky, off-beat, throwaway, preposterous . . . it's joyously ridiculous." Ruth Gordon (who curiously also starred in "Where's Poppa?") is excellent again in a completely different and challenging comedy role. BEN KERN of the Minneapolis Sunday Tribune said "Ruth Gordon is on-the-button as Maude." Co-starring with her is Bud Cort, an exciting young talent. See "Harold and Maude" tonight at 7:35 and 9:40

EXTRA-SPECIAL SHORT SUBJECT!
"DE DUVE" ("The Dove") At 7:15 & 9:25
(Will Jones wrote about it in his column Monday, March 20)

The advertising folks worked hard to position Harold and Maude as the next Where's Poppa?, even going so far as to use a headshot of Ruth Gordon from Where's Poppa? to solidify the connection.

The (Short) Movie Before the Movie

De Düva is a delightful and loving send-up of the films of Ingmar Bergman – employing arty black-and-white photography, subtitles and dialogue that sounds just enough like Swedish that it takes some audience members a while to realize it's actually just *Swedish-sounding* English.

It was written by Sidney Davis (who plays Death in the film) and directed by Anthony Lover and George Coe (who plays Victor).

Pamela Burrell, who played Inga in the short, remembered the first time she saw *De Düva* with an audience.

"It was playing with a movie called *The Fox* with Sandy Dennis," Burrell recalled. "It

opened the program, and the film started. And it was very quiet. Up until George opened his mouth and started to talk. Then a few people – not the whole audience, but a few people – started to laugh. And a lot of the other people started to shush them.

"I couldn't believe it, because to my ear, it is so obvious that we're speaking English. I don't know how it took so long. But it was amazing. And then, of course, they caught on. It was a marvelous experience."

... I had a terrible dream

The Westgate's assistant manager, Randy Greene, said there was a similar response to most screenings of *De Düva* at the theater.

"About two or three minutes into it, people get it: He's not talking Swedish," Greene told me. "Then they all start breaking out laughing. They get the joke finally. But it takes a few minutes."

The original idea had been to make a feature film in four segments, each one parodying a different country's style of filmmaking: Truffaut/France, Fellini/Italy, Kurosawa/Japan and Bergman/Sweden.

"We took this idea to Paramount," recalled co-director Anthony Lover. "And they said, 'Don't do this. Really, don't do this. You're talking about some of the greatest filmmakers, and who the hell are you guys?'"

Lover and partner George Coe decided to make the film with their own money and the help of

Cigar?

One point wins.

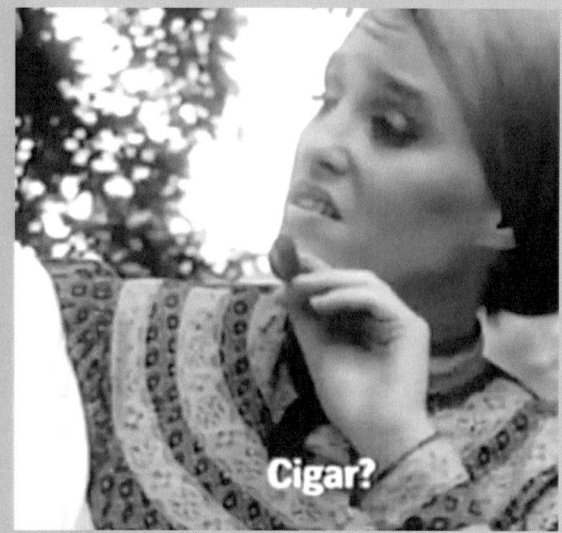

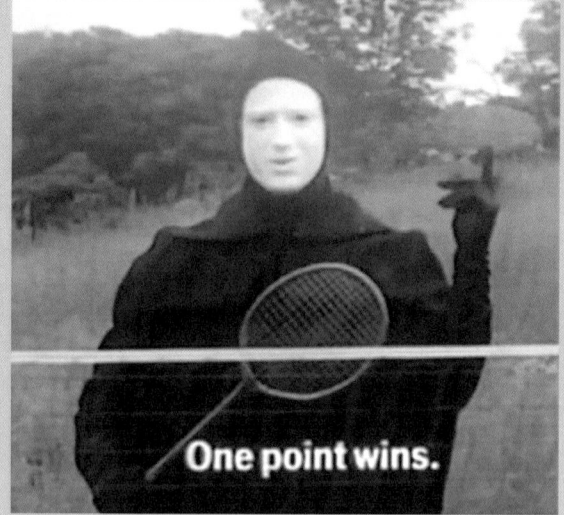

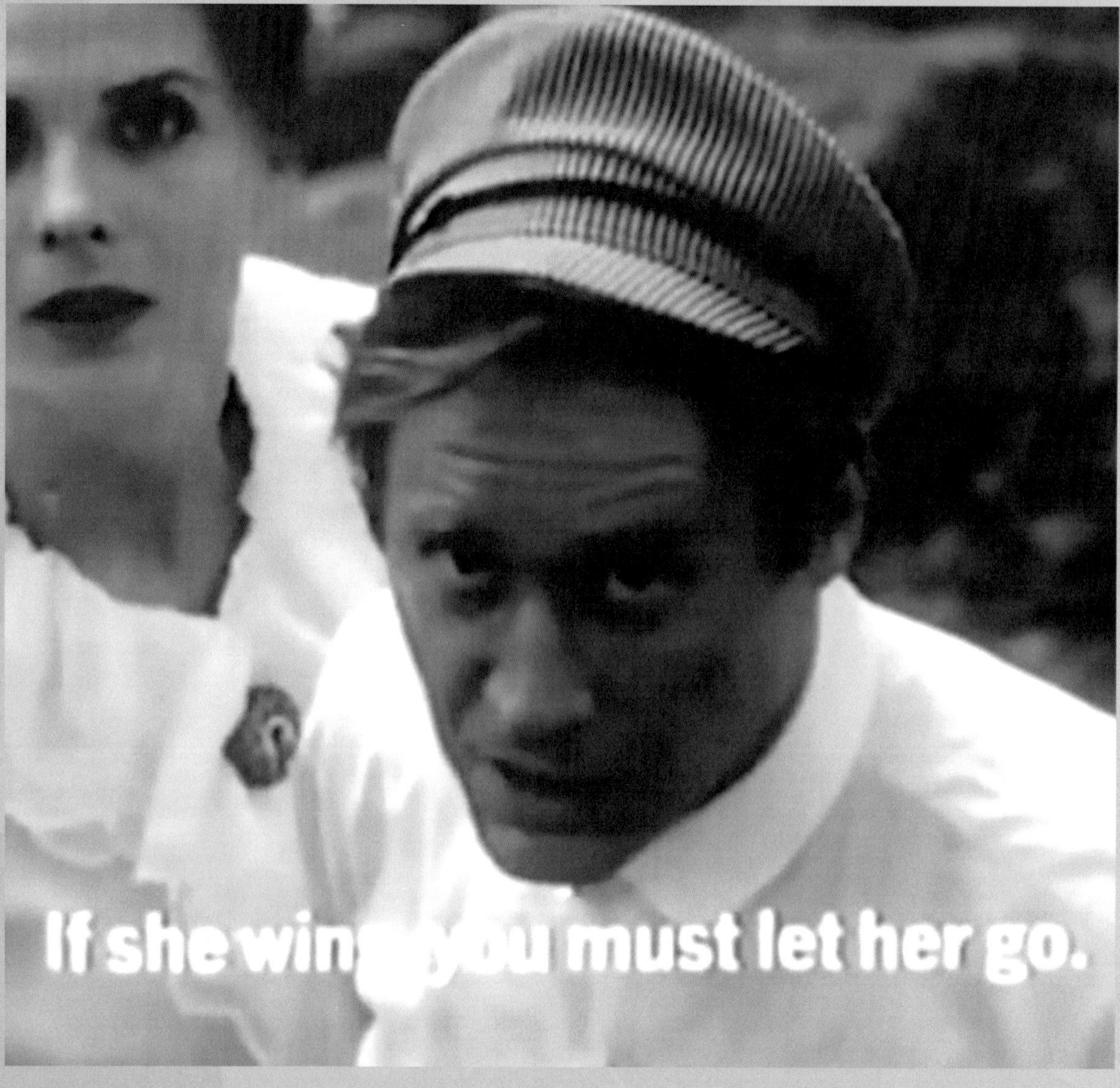
If she win you must let her go.

a couple investors. "And so," Lover recalled, "the luck of the draw, we decided to do Bergman first."

However, the short became so famous that they never attempted the other three stories. A *New York Times* film critic, who snuck into a cast and crew screening of the finished film, recommended it to director Miloš Forman, who insisted the short accompany a film of his that was just about to open at the Film Society in Lincoln Center.

From that debut, *De Düva* went on to win awards all over the world and was even nominated for an Academy Award for Best Live Action Short Subject.

Co-director Anthony Lover looked back on the experience fondly. "It's just interesting," he said, "how when you have a vision and you decide to do something – even though everyone tells you not to do it – you go ahead and do it. And then afterwards everyone says, 'Oh, yeah, it's great. Wonderful!'"

YEAR ONE

THE EARLY INTEREST IN the popular run of *Harold and Maude* (and *De Düva*) at The Westgate looked like it might easily equal the popularity of *The Twelve Chairs*. And then, as the weeks when on, it appeared to be gaining on the love for *Where's Poppa?*

"In the beginning, the younger people were coming," assistant manager Randy Greene recalled. "Probably college age, maybe a little older than that, but young people came. But it did change over time, when you'd see an older audience mix in with it."

Theater manager Ralph Watschke agreed with that assessment, telling local film critic

Harold and Maude at the Westgate

The biggest advertising challenge was to come up with new ways to tell newspaper readers how many weeks Harold and Maude had been playing at The Westgate.

Don Morrison that "the attendance during the first year ran in cycles, beginning with the sophisticated older set, then the university contingent, a run of senior citizens, 'a short hippy phase' and then increasingly the mostly high school and college crowd."

"We did take surveys once in a while about who had seen the movie before," Greene told me. "And a lot of times it was half – or more than half – had seen it before. And you'd get comments like 'I've seen it five times, but I'm dragging so-and-so here with me to see it because they've got to see this thing.'"

Few people disliked the show, Watschke told *Tribune* columnist Peg Meier, telling her that "he could count on the fingers of his two hands the number of people who told the theater staff it offended them."

However, after a few months, news of the oddly long run at The Westgate was starting to get around. A series of ads appeared in the Detroit Free Press in September of 1972.

One ad read, in part:

"The *Harold and Maude* success story began in Minneapolis 28 weeks ago, when the film comedy opened at the suburban Westgate Theatre to smash business. Despite good reviews, *Harold and Maude* was a box-office disappointment in most cities (including Detroit) in the holiday season competitive scramble.

"The Westgate Theatre felt the film was too good not to give it a second shot, so *Harold and Maude* was brought back in a second 'first-run' engagement that began March 22, 1972. The film has grossed a sensational $125,000 and it's still running after 28 weeks. The Westgate thinks word-of-mouth advertising will keep it going until next Christmas.

"The Studio 4 Theatre is happy to report the film is enjoying the same success here as in Minneapolis. Most of our patrons also appreciate the humor of Minneapolis, showing New York, Detroit and the rest of the country how to get it done."

Harold and Maude at the Westgate

"HAROLD and MAUDE" says: AS MINNEAPOLIS GOES, SO GOES THE NATION!

The HAROLD AND MAUDE success story began in Minneapolis 24 weeks ago when the film comedy opened at the suburban Westgate Theatre to smash business.

Despite good reviews, HAROLD AND MAUDE was a boxoffice disappointment in most cities (including Detroit) in the holiday season competitive scramble.

Paramount Pictures was ready to consign HAROLD AND MAUDE to the television scrap heap until Minneapolis entered the scene. The Westgate Theatre felt the film was too good not to give it a second shot, so HAROLD AND MAUDE was brought back in a second "first-run" engagement which began March 22, 1972.

The film has grossed a sensational $125,000 and it's still running after 24 weeks. The Westgate thinks word-of-mouth advertising will keep it going till next Christmas.

The Studio 4 Theatre, which opened HAROLD AND MAUDE Aug. 30, is happy to report the film is enjoying the same success here as in Minneapolis.

Most of our patrons agree with Free Press critic Susan Stark who called HAROLD AND MAUDE "the most easy-to-take comedy of the year" and who picked it as one of the year's 10 best films.

They also appreciate the humor of Minneapolis showing New York, Detroit and the rest of the country how to get it done.

Now! STUDIO 4 — 394 So. Woodward in Birmingham — 645-0777

Detroit had fun with the idea that any city (including Detroit or New York) might actually learn something from Minneapolis.

"HAROLD AND MAUDE" says: TODAY MINNEAPOLIS — TOMORROW THE WORLD!

The HAROLD AND MAUDE success story began in Minneapolis 28 weeks ago when the film comedy opened at the suburban Westgate Theatre to smash business.

Despite good reviews, HAROLD AND MAUDE was a boxoffice disappointment in most cities (including Detroit) in the holiday season competitive scramble.

Paramount Pictures was ready to consign HAROLD AND MAUDE to the television scrap heap until Minneapolis entered the scene. The Westgate Theatre felt the film was too good not to give it a second shot, so HAROLD AND MAUDE was brought back in a second "first-run" engagement which began March 22, 1972.

The film has grossed a sensational $125,000 and it's still running after 24 weeks. The Westgate thinks word-of-mouth advertising will keep it going till next Christmas.

The Studio 4 Theatre, which opened HAROLD AND MAUDE Aug. 30, is happy to report the film is enjoying the same success here as in Minneapolis.

Most of our patrons agree with Free Press critic Susan Stark who called HAROLD AND MAUDE "the most easy-to-take comedy of the year" and who picked it as one of the year's 10 best films.

They also appreciate the humor of Minneapolis showing New York, Detroit and the rest of the country how to get it done.

Held Over 5th Week! *(It's catching on here, too)* STUDIO 4 — 394 So. Woodward in Birmingham — 645-0777

The Super Fan – Doug Strand

'MAUDE' AND SUPER-FAN — Actress Ruth Gordon came to the Westgate Theater, 3903 Sunnyside Av., Edina, last night to launch the second-year continuous run of her film "Harold and Maude." Greeting her was Douglas Strand, a St. Paul judicial clerk, who thinks the film is something special. He has seen it about 70 times. Miss Gordon, an Academy Award winner, heard about the suburban theater's long run of the film at a Hollywood party. She thought it would be fun to join the anniversary party.

Minneapolis Star Photo by Jack Gillis

Just about any article in a Minneapolis or St. Paul paper about the long run of Harold and Maude at The Westgate would not be complete without a mention of Doug Strand and his love of the film.

Super Fan Doug Strand's favorite scene in the movie. (It's also Vivian Pickles' favorite scene.)

During the long run of *Harold and Maude* in the Twin Cities, Doug Strand became somewhat legendary for the number of times he saw the film.

Doug, a municipal court clerk, was frequently mentioned in newspaper articles about the movie, and was invited to join Ruth Gordon when she came to town for the first-year anniversary at The Westgate.

After seeing the film for the first time, Doug went back almost immediately for a second viewing. "It just hit me. I kept going back," he said.

"I went back," he told me, because "I was friends with the woman who was about 50 years older than I was at the time. And she died. I wasn't trying to commit suicide to get attention from my mother. But I saw some similarities there that were helping me get over Beryl's death – similarities between us and Harold and Maude. She was 65 and I was 20. She died on her 65th birthday of a heart attack. I was the same height, weight and age as Harold."

And so, Doug just got into the habit of seeing *Harold and Maude*.

"It kind of became addictive," he said. "I would tell myself I wouldn't go, and then at seven o'clock I'd say, 'Well, what the hell.' I was living at the time in the little guest house behind my sister's house. It was only, I don't know, five miles maybe to the theater."

Although he hasn't watched the film beginning to end since the soundtrack album came out, even today Doug still has a favorite scene: "When Harold pretends to shoot himself. His mother is reading from the National Computer Dating Service. Where he tips over in the chair. That still tickles me."

Repeated viewings also helped him discover one of the few continuity errors in the film. On around his 85th viewing, he noticed "when Maude 'borrows' a truck to transport a sickly city tree to the woods, the truck window is sometimes shut and sometimes halfway open."

The time Doug spent at the one-year anniversary with Ruth Gordon led to a friendship which lasted until her death, which included visits to her home on Martha's Vineyard or trips to see her on-stage.

"I saw her a lot," he recalled. "Every time they came to Minnesota. When they would go on *Twin Cities Live* or *Good Company*. I'd take the time off work and go every time either she or (her husband) Garson were on that show."

He also traveled to see her on-stage, first in Boston (in *Dreyfus In Rehearsal*, which Clive Barnes, in his *New York Times* review, said "is a kind of *Fiddler on the Roof* without the fiddle.") He also travelled to New York to see her in *Mrs. Warren's Profession*.

"I drove to New York to see that play," he recalled. "I walked into Ruth's dressing room. I had sent her a postcard wishing her luck. The postcard was on her mirror. The only other thing that was stuck on the mirror was a telegram from Katharine Hepburn, wishing her the best."

Throughout their years' long friendship, Doug was always struck by one thing about Ruth Gordon: "What you saw on TV, what you saw in movies, it wasn't even acting. It was her."

Doug Strand and friend Ruth Gordon.

The ONE-YEAR ANNIVERSARY

As the film's run moved into 1973, it became clear that *Harold and Maude* would absolutely make it to the one-year mark … and perhaps beyond.

To celebrate the landmark event, the folks at General Cinema invited Ruth Gordon to town for the one-year anniversary. They also invited Super Fan Doug Strand to act as her escort, as a sort of Bud Cort substitute.

"Somebody from General Cinema called me," Doug remembered. "That was when they were gearing up to do the first anniversary at The Westgate. And they asked me if I wanted to have dinner with Ruth Gordon. And of course, I said yes."

Free cake and coffee … plus, here's a map of where we are, in case you've never been here before but still want to stop by.

Harold and Maude at the Westgate

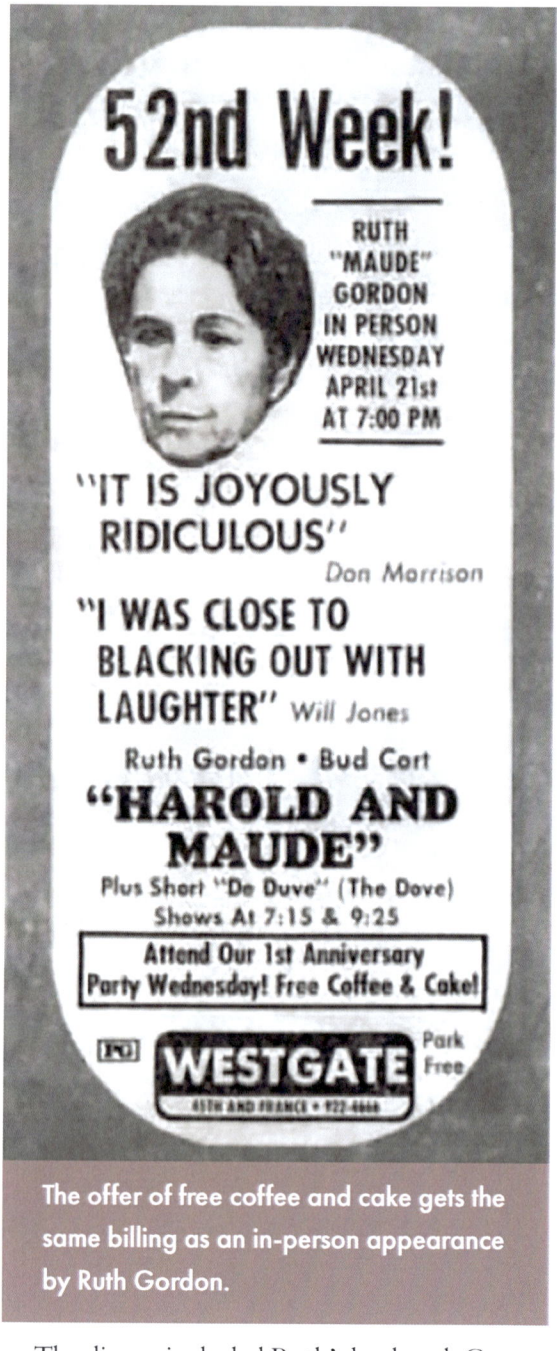

The offer of free coffee and cake gets the same billing as an in-person appearance by Ruth Gordon.

The dinner included Ruth's husband, Garson Kanin, The Westgate's manager, Ralph Watschke, as well as *Star Tribune* critic Don Morrison.

According to Morrison, "Studio biggies had scoffed at the idea of a suburb appearance by Ms. Gordon when the theater people proposed it. But the Oscar-winning actress happened to hear about the idea while at a Hollywood party and was delighted to accept."

Gordon was invited to fly to Minneapolis to appear at The Westgate and cut a giant cake with the help of Douglas Strand, who, according to Morrison, "certainly has earned the co-slicer role."

For his part, Doug did not take the event lightly, even going so far as to do some last-minute research on Gordon's work and career.

"I made a lot of preparation to meet her after I was invited to that dinner," he told me. "I went to the library, looked up and copied every review of every play she'd ever been in that was covered by Alexander Wolcott and

Ruth Gordon interviewed, with her biggest fan (Doug Strand) in the background.

Ruth Gordon (and Doug Strand) cut that cake which had been promised in all the ads.

Ruth Gordon in Seventeen...

...and Thornton Wilder's adaptation of A Doll's House.

The New York Times. I read all of them. I didn't want to look stupid."

This wasn't Ruth Gordon's first trip to the area. She had been in Minneapolis fifty-seven years before (in 1916) as understudy to Maude Adams in *The Little Minister*, and then back three years later playing the lead in *Seventeen*. She even played Nora in Thornton Wilder's adaptation of *A Doll's House* in 1938.

From the perspective of The Westgate Theater's staff, it was an exciting – if overwhelming – event.

"We didn't have advanced tickets at that point," assistant manager Randy Greene recalled. "So, when I came to work that day there was a mass of people out front. We knew we were going to sell the place out. It's only about 500 seats or thereabouts, but it was just a mass of people outside. It was fun. But we turned a lot of people away."

Don Morrison concurred. "I arrived at 6:30 p.m. to avoid the last-minute press for Ms. Gordon's 7 p.m. appearance," he wrote. "There already was a line down the block. Theater manager Ralph Watschke said that young enthusiasts had shown up with blankets at 4 p.m. and settled on the sidewalk to wait."

Morrison then went on to recount the events of the evening. "When the tiny, 5-foot star arrived at the theater, a joyous roar went up from the crowd packed in the lobby, despite ushers' efforts to move them into the theater," he wrote. "She and Strand symbolically cut a birthday cake.

"After the patrons were more or less seated," Morrison continued, "she walked down the aisle to the stage. I've seen standing ovations in my time and I've heard the rabbit-squeals of teeny-boppers when their latest imaginary

Harold and Maude at the Westgate

Ruth takes a moment to autograph her book in The Westgate's small art gallery space.

sex-object appears. This was different – not just celebrity excitement or pubescent cult cries, but a sweeping great wave of open affection.

"She mounted the stage and in a cracked voice started singing *If You Want to Sing Out*, the movie theme, to which the kids of all ages clapped along.

"'Remember the last words in *Harold and Maude*?' she asked. 'They were: "I love you."' Kids in the front row held up a big cloth banner: 'Sing Out, Ruth!' And others came up to give her daisies – the film's symbolic flower.

"Later, at an after-triumph supper at the Kings' Inn," Morrison concluded, "a group of teenage girls, who had somehow tracked her down, waited in the foyer. They did not merely want her autograph; they wanted to kiss her. So did I."

Minneapolis Tribune columnist Will Jones also reported on the event. "When fans suggest that she has perhaps become the films' leading batty-old-lady specialist," Jones reported, "she makes the same defense of the mother she played in *Where's Poppa?* and, for that matter, the mother in *Lord Love a Duck*. 'To me, they aren't far-out at all,' she said. 'There's a little of me in them, and I believe in them. Lord knows, anybody who lives an interesting life at all is not far-out.'"

That evening's second show, according to Greene, was less bombastic. "The crowd was half full at the most or something like that," he told me. "Most people wanted to see it with Maude."

For her part, Ruth Gordon appeared as delighted to see her audience as they had been to see her. In a telegram she sent to the folks at General Cinema (later reprinted in the newspaper), she expressed her appreciation.

"I'm still sailing on clouds toward Never-Never Land," she wrote, "from the most

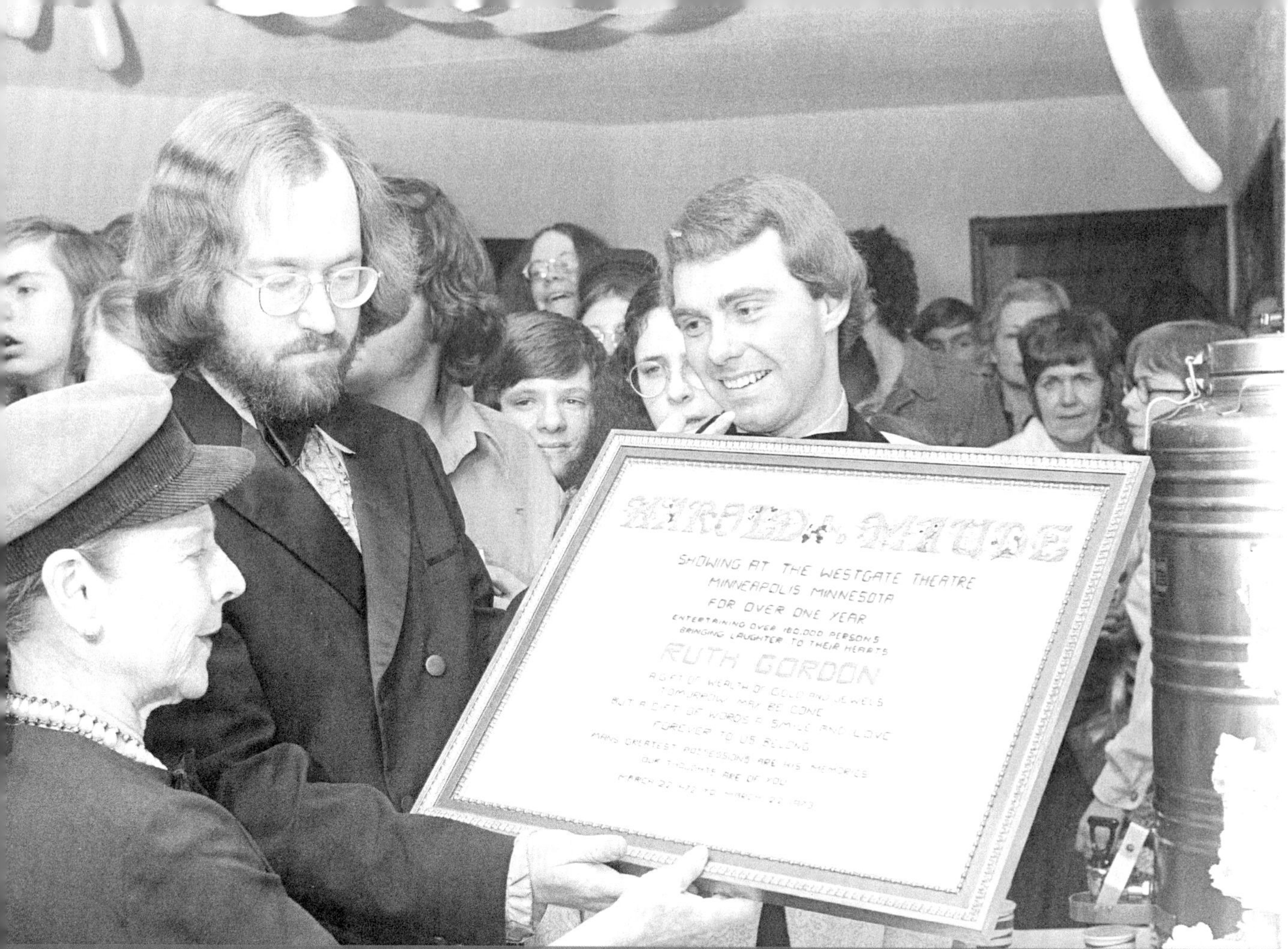

Ruth Gordon is presented with an embroidered plaque by The Westgate's manager, Ralph Watschke, as Doug Strand looks on. The plaque reads: Harold and Maude. Showing at The Westgate Theatre Minneapolis, Minnesota for over one year. Entertaining over 100,000 persons, bringing laughter to their hearts. Ruth Gordon: a gift of wealth, of gold and jewels / Tomorrow may be gone / But a gift of words, a smile and love / Forever to us belong. Man's greatest possessions are his memories. Our thoughts are of you. March 22, 1972 to March 22, 1973.

marvelous, magical reception that all the people of Minneapolis gave me on the first anniversary of *Harold and Maude*. The warmth and wonderful reception was unlike anything I have ever experienced before. I'll keep my fingers crossed that you'll invite me back for the second anniversary."

Happily, Ruth's wish would come true.

THANK YOU, RUTH GORDON!

WESTERN UNION **Telegram**

PMS TED MANN
GCC-MANN THEATRES
16 N. 7TH STREET
MINNEAPOLIS, MINNESOTA 55403

.... PLEASE DELIVER ....

DEAR TED

I'M STILL SAILING ON CLOUDS TOWARD NEVER-NEVER LAND FROM THE MOST MARVELOUS, MAGICAL RECEPTION THAT YOU AND YOUR ASSOCIATES AND ALL THE PEOPLE OF MINNEAPOLIS GAVE TO ME ON THE FIRST ANNIVERSARY OF "HAROLD AND MAUDE." THE WARMTH AND WONDERFUL RECEPTION WAS UNLIKE ANYTHING I HAVE EVER EXPERIENCED BEFORE AND I AM SO GRATEFUL TO YOU, BOB MILLER, YOUR ENTIRE STAFF AT THE WESTGATE THEATRE AND THE MOST GLORIOUS GROUP OF PEOPLE EVER. I HOPE WE CAN STAY FOREVER IN MINNEAPOLIS — GARSON AND I THANK YOU FROM THE BOTTOM OF OUR HEARTS. I'LL KEEP MY FINGERS CROSSED THAT YOU'LL INVITE ME BACK FOR THE SECOND ANNIVERSARY.

LOVE,
RUTH GORDON

"HAROLD & MAUDE" PG Color
Plus Short "De Duve"
Shows At 7:15 & 9:25
WESTGATE
45TH AND FRANCE • 922-4666
Park Free

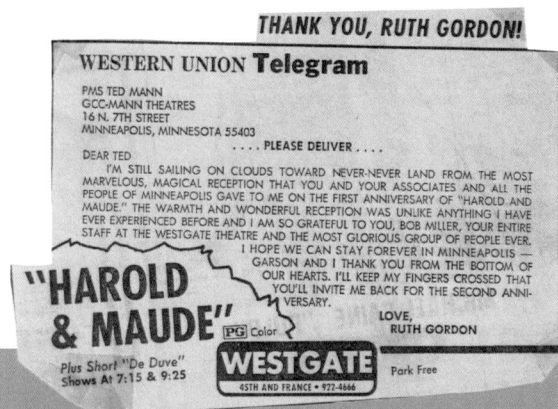

Ruth Gordon's Thank You telegram.

YEAR TWO

Harold and Maude just went on and on (and on) at The Westgate.

When the run hit 70 weeks, *Minneapolis Tribune* writer Irv Letofsky reported the theater had sold 275,000 tickets so far and although attendance had dipped about fifteen percent, "the end is nowhere in sight."

And so the theater staff settled into the groove of serving the same movie night after night. The publicity photos outside the theater started to fade, and theater manager Ralph Watschke admitted to one reporter that he was afraid he'd forgotten how to change the name of the movie on the marquee. But, despite that, he still liked the film. "I'd be totally bananas by now if I didn't."

The continued repetition of the same movie night after night did provide one consistent cue for the staff.

"One of the great practical things about *Harold and Maude* was the five minute 'WHAT!,'" recalled employee Amy Eisenstadt.

Harold, seconds away from alerting The Westgate staff that there's just about five minutes left in the movie.

The Westgate inches up on The Downtown Mann Theater's 95-week record, with The Sound of Music.

"Harold yells 'What!' about 5 minutes before the end of the movie," she explained. "It was super easy to hear in the lobby. That was our cue to quit goofing off and get ready to open the doors and generally get ready for the people to be leaving the theater."

Even the folks back in Hollywood were struggling to explain the success of the film.

"I remember discussing it with staff and not knowing why," recalled Charles Glenn, the Global Head of Marketing for Paramount. "Why would people continue to populate The Westgate Theater in Minneapolis for years? And where would they draw an audience from? And then how do you fill those seats up? 365 days? I mean, it's extraordinary. But there it was."

The next landmark date for the film was surpassing 95 weeks.

"At the 95th week," explained assistant manager Randy Greene, "*Harold and Maude* beat the record for the longest running movie

Until Harold and Maude came along, The Sound of Music had set the record for the longest running movie in Minnesota.

Harold and Maude at the Westgate

in Minnesota. Before that it was *The Sound of Music*. Back in the 60s, it played at one of the downtown theaters for 95 weeks. So, *Harold and Maude* beat *The Sound of Music*.

The downside to that long run, however, was the wear and tear it put on the film print.

"It got really chewed up, scratched, and splices and stuff were in it," Greene remembered. "We would every now and then ask for a new print to be shipped in. At one point, Paramount said, 'We have no new prints anymore. We have nothing.' And so they said, 'We'll send you two or three prints and you pick the best reels out of the ones we send you.' And so, we went through, and we picked the best reels out of the prints that they sent."

And before they knew it, it was time for the next landmark date.

Tribune cartoonist Richard Guindon offered his own take on the assumed staff morale at The Westgate during the film's extraordinary run.

"Thank you for calling the Westgate Theater. Do you have a few minutes to chat? We don't get many calls . . ."

The TWO-YEAR ANNIVERSARY

IF ONE STAR OF *Harold and Maude* could appear for the first anniversary, the folks at General Cinema concluded that two stars would be perfect for the film's second year anniversary celebration at The Westgate.

The call went out, and both Ruth Gordon and Bud Cort agreed to make the trek to Minneapolis in March 1974.

This is the point where the book's author will insert himself into the story, if only briefly. Thanks to *Minneapolis Tribune* writer Irv Letofsky, I was able to join him for a dinner with Bud Cort at a popular local steak house, Harry's, the night before the big celebration.

Letofsky reported on the dinner the next day (not mentioning me, of course), writing "Bud is strongly committed to a career of

Dinner with Bud Cort at Harry's restaurant. You'll have to take my word for it, but I am seated just to Bud's right.

'anything that's good,' which might explain why he has rejected several movie and TV scripts. Upon deciding to make this trip, he had his agent start proceedings to get him into the Guthrie Theater company, and one of his first stops yesterday ('It blew my mind') was to stop in on Vineland Place and meet the people."

Coincidentally, Bud just missed his *Harold and Maude* co-star, Eric Christmas (The Priest). Christmas had recently directed *I, Said the Fly* during The Guthrie's 1973-74 season,

No mention of cake in the second anniversary ad.

Harold and Maude at the Westgate

Eric Christmas at The Guthrie Theatre in The Caretaker (above) and in Loot (below, with Mark Lamos and Cara Duff-MacCormick) during the theatre's 1975-76 season.

and would return as an actor in *The Caretaker* and *Loot* during the 1975-76 season.

On the big anniversary day, with my trusty Super 8mm camera in hand, I followed Ruth and Bud as they made their way from press event to press event (they traveled in a limo; I tried to keep up via local bus service). The frame grabs on this and the next two pages document their day.

First stop, filming an early morning TV interview, which placed them in the front row seats at The Westgate Theater. The interviewer was local TV personality Nancy Nelson.

Then they headed downtown, for another TV appearance, this time at WCCO-TV with Bill Carlson (spouse of their first interviewer, Nancy Nelson).

Ruth and Bud (still in the car) arrive, under the watchful eye of theater manager Ralph Watschke.

Ruth Gordon returns to The Westgate lobby.

Bud recognizes the kid behind the camera.

Final touchups before the camera rolls with interviewer Nancy Nelson.

After the interview, Ruth and Bud signed autographs and photos – including a couple for me.

The first public outing for the pair was advertised as "Have Tea With Harold and Maude." The event, held in the auditorium at the top of Dayton's downtown department store, was an immediate sell-out.

Hosted by popular *Minneapolis Tribune* columnist Barbara Flanagan, the event (as reported by writer Nancy Livingston for the

Harold and Maude at the Westgate

Ruth graciously signing photos.

competing *St. Paul Dispatch)*, began with something of an uproar.

"The ruckus came about," Livingston wrote, "when Dayton's officials initially told about 150 persons that the Skyroom dining room was filled and they could not get in to see Miss Gordon and Bud Cort. Loud cries of 'We want to see Harold and Maude' brought results, however, and the 150 extras were allowed to file in free of charge. (Everybody else paid $1)."

Livingston went on to report: "Asked if she liked being type cast. Miss Gordon said forcefully, 'Whether or not you are typed is beside the point. The important thing is to get a job. Then you have got to deliver. The most dignified thing in the world is to earn a living.'

"Cort, who hasn't worked in a movie since *Harold and Maude* was made three and a half years ago, disagreed. He said he's been offered a couple of parts – such as a man who falls in love with a boa constrictor. And another as a baby who crawls around in a crib for the entire feature length. He said he turned them down because 'I'm waiting for someone to take a chance on me.'"

On the WCCO-TV set with veteran celebrity interviewer Bill Carlson.

Livingston's report concluded with a quick mention of the film's Super Fan: "Red-haired Doug Strand, who has gone through mounds of popcorn and dozens of candy bars while watching the movie 156 different times, received a round of applause Wednesday for his achievement."

Later, Ruth and Bud arrived at The Westgate for the first show of the evening.

Then it was into the auditorium and onto the stage in front of the sell-out crowd.

Ruth spoke first, delighting the audience

That's right, Ruth Gordon and Bud Cort, your favorite stars, from Minneapolis' favorite movie, "Harold and Maude", are coming to our town to help celebrate the start of the third year of their movie at the Westgate theatre. Barbara Flanagan will host the tea and the question and answer session where you'll be able to quiz the stars on just about anything. The tea is this Wednesday, March 20 at 3:30 p.m. in our Downtown Minneapolis 12 Floor Sky Room. Admission is $1 . . . which isn't a lot for talking to the stars.

Have tea with Harold and Maude
Wednesday, March 20
at 3:30 p.m.

DAYTON'S

Ruth Gordon and columnist Barbara Flanagan.

Tea with Harold and Maude. Admission was just one dollar, which as the ad pointed out, isn't a lot for talking to the stars.

Bud Cort joins the ladies on stage.

(and Bud) with her oft-repeated story of her response when director Hal Ashby said he was going to London to interview other actresses for the part of Maude ("Well, to hell with him, I thought!").

She then went on to say: "I'm glad to be here. You know, it's a great thing to be in a place where something goes right. And for two years, at The Westgate Theatre, things have gone right for *Harold and Maude*. And tonight, it includes Bud and me."

Bud wrapped up the short appearance with an emotional message to the audience: "I think there's nothing anybody can say except thank

Someone must have remembered how to change the letters on the marquee after all.

Harold and Maude at the Westgate

Bud receives an ovation in the lobby...

...while Ruth receives a daisy in the theater's small art gallery area.

Bud and Ruth making short speeches in front of the curtain on the stage.

you all for believing in the film and making this probably one of the most touching moments of my life, and I'm sure for Ruth too. She said it. And God bless you all."

The author's signed photos from Ruth and Bud.

The Protest

The theater was a little better prepared for the crowds who showed up for the second-year anniversary screening. But they weren't prepared for the protesters.

Over the previous two years, the staff had received numerous objections about the film's long run at The Westgate.

"We got a lot of complaints on the phone," assistant manager Randy Greene recalled.

Bud and Ruth arrive and pose in front of the protesters.

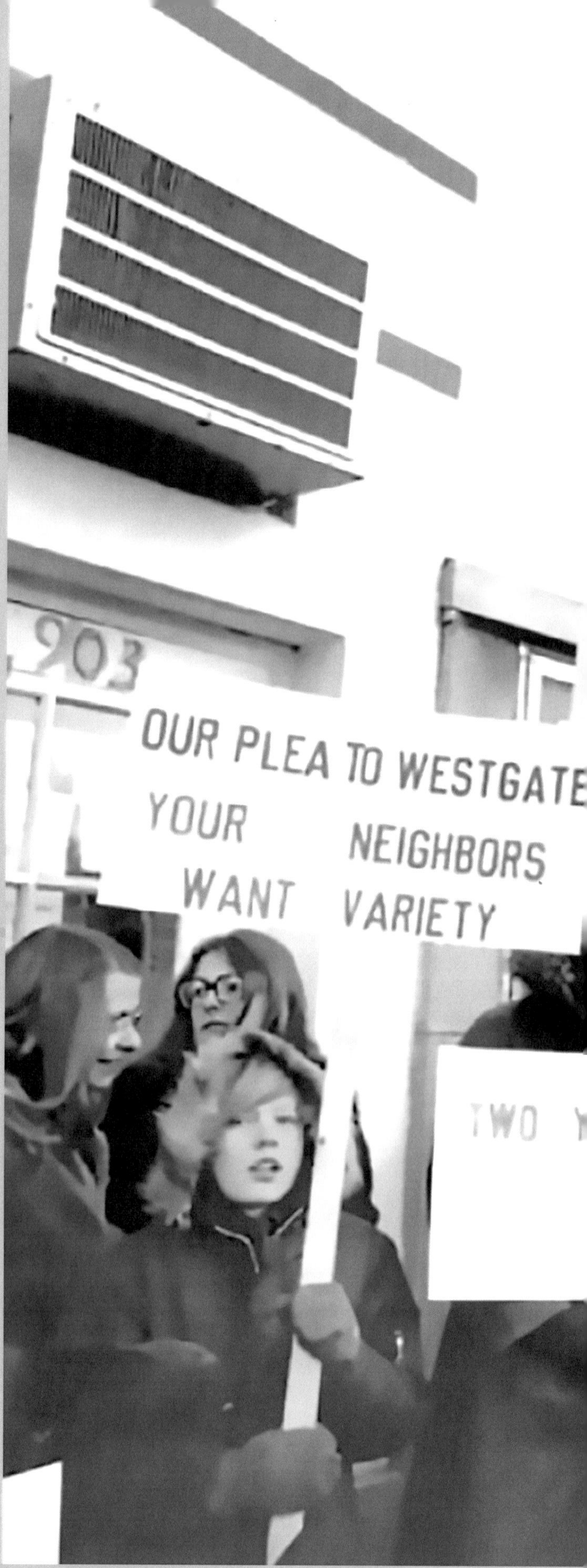

The protest, spearheaded by Morningside housewife Betty Owen, was in good fun, but they were also serious: We want a new movie!

"And some people would come in, in person and say, 'Change the movie.' And all you could say was, 'People keep coming. We can't pull it because we're making money out of it. You have to keep the movie that makes money.'"

Those complaints came to life that night, in the form of neighbors marching in front of the theater, bearing picket signs, expressing sentiments like "Two Years is Too Much," "Your Neighbors Want Variety," and "Why Must the Show Go On and On and On?"

As reported in the *Minneapolis Star*: "A group of Edina residents picketed The Westgate Theater yesterday to protest the 104-week showing of *Harold and Maude*. Mrs. Henry (Betty) Owen, said that many neighborhood residents would like to patronize the theater, but they won't unless the movie changes.

"Mrs. Owen said she'd called the theater twice to complain, but was told *Harold and Maude* would continue as long as it drew customers. Mrs. Owen said she'd like to see as a substitute anything but 'hardcore pornography.' She hasn't seen *Harold and Maude* but has read four reviews which didn't make the movie sound like something she'd want to see, Mrs. Owen said."

The group chose that evening for their protest "because there was an occasion and people were going to be there," recalled Betty's husband, Henry Owen.

"It was the right moment to do it," Henry told me. "Because there would be attention focused on it. I think they just realized it's been two years since we've been able to send our kids to a movie there. I think they saw it as our neighborhood resource and for two years we haven't been able to use it. So, they just decided to do that."

Although the protest received a lot of press coverage, Henry was quick to downplay its intent as well as its impact.

"It wasn't a monumental thing," he said. "It wasn't like they went down to the theater and nailed Ninety-Five Theses to the door. I think they were having some fun and they just wanted to do it. And they did it."

The END COMES

FOLLOWING THE ANNIVERSARY CELEBRATION, there was a subtle but noticeable shift at the theater.

"After the second anniversary, there was a different feeling," assistant manager Randy Greene recalled. "We had two shows that night. Both shows were very busy and very full. But the next few weeks after that, it just felt different. You could see the energy was running out."

Attendance began to dwindle. "We got so few people for a show," recalled employee Amy Eisenstadt, "that often only two people would work a shift – one person at the ticket booth, who would also take the ticket, and one behind the candy counter."

With sales dropping, the folks at General Cinema made a decision.

"They announced at the end of March, or the beginning of April, that they were going to quit running it," Greene explained. "And immediately the big, big crowds came back. And then they said, 'Well, okay, we'll extend it.' And they extended it for almost a month or so before they finally pulled it. And those last few weeks, people were coming back, getting nostalgic about it."

Minneapolis Tribune writer Irv Letofsky announced the end of the era under the headline "*Harold and Maude* is Finally Leaving."

"After 115 weeks, two days and $425,000, *Harold and Maude* will close Thursday night at The Westgate Theater in Edina," Letofsky wrote. "Into its place will go the French farce *The Tall Blond Man with One Black Shoe*."

Letofsky went on to report: "Although *Harold and Maude* audiences – mostly recidivists – have

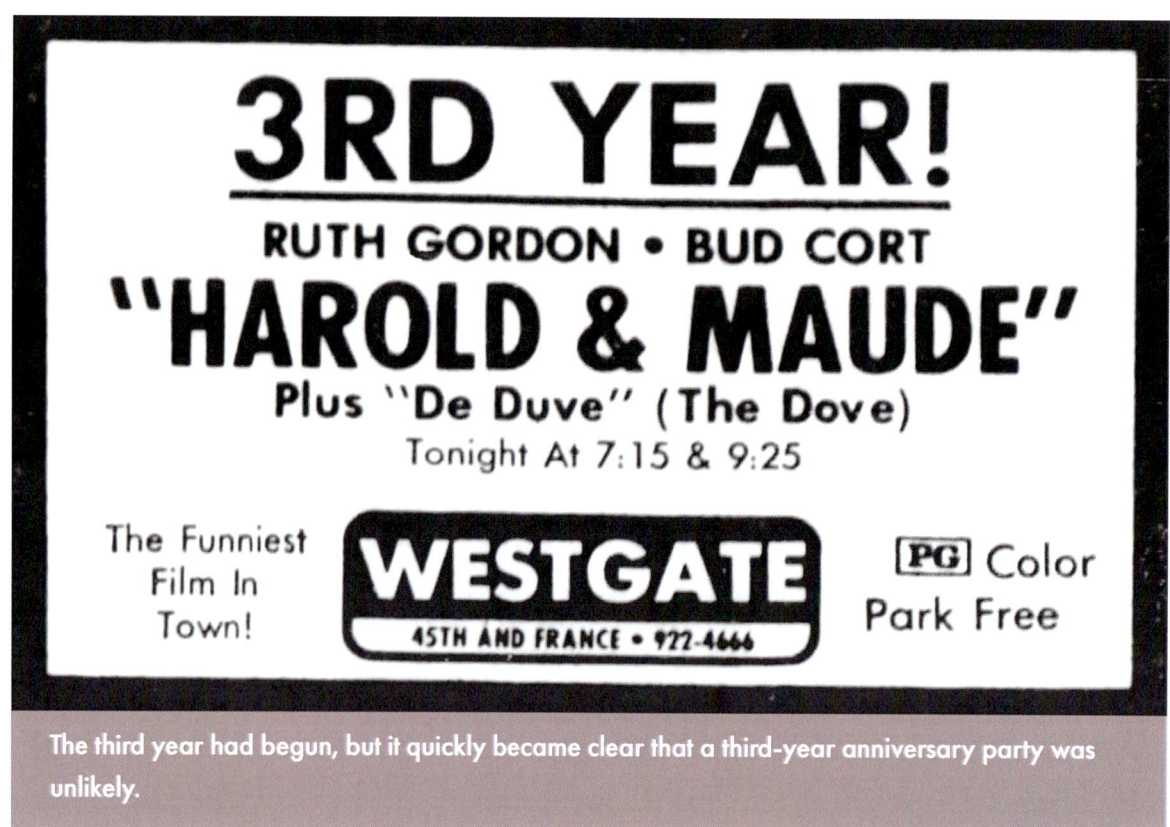

The third year had begun, but it quickly became clear that a third-year anniversary party was unlikely.

Harold and Maude at the Westgate

Despite a slight bump in attendance, it was decided that the Harold and Maude era was coming to a close.

been falling off, the last two to three weeks have been pretty good, according to theater officials. But *Tall Blond Man* was scheduled and promoted to go in, and the decision was made to drop *Harold and Maude*."

The final night for the film was memorialized by *Minneapolis Tribune* writer Bob Lundegaard: "At 11:07 p.m. Thursday, a boy named Harold strummed his banjo and gamboled along a California cliff for the 1,957th time, while an audience of 170 at the Westgate Theater rose and applauded. It was the last scene of the last showing of *Harold and Maude* at The Westgate after a record run of 115 weeks and one day."

Lundegaard went on to report: "'It's the

The number of exclamation points after "Hurry" (five) matched the number of days left for Harold and Maude at The Westgate.

Harold and Maude at the Westgate

end of an era,' said Douglas Strand, a 22-year-old court clerk from St. Paul who did more than anyone else to keep the zany comedy running for more than two years. 'I feel kind of empty inside.' Strand saw the film for the 164th time at 7:30, then waited in the lobby for the short subjects to finish before going back in for No. 165."

Although he wasn't scheduled to work that night, manager Ralph Watschke came by before the show ended. "I was riding around on my motorcycle," he explained, "and the picture just kind of drew me back here."

Protest leader Betty Owen wasn't at the final screening, as she had never seen the movie, but she was thrilled the era had finally come to an end. "I have a thing about funerals," she explained. 'I read reviews of the movie in the paper, and I guess the whole movie is about funerals.' However, she confirmed that she had plans to see the new movie once it opened."

Doug Strand, who had continued his long-distance relationship with Ruth Gordon, told Lundegaard the actress had recently phoned.

"She telephoned him last week with some good news," Lundegaard wrote. "The movie was about to re-open in New York, where it had bombed in 1971, with newspaper ads reminding the New York rubes that 'Minneapolis is three years ahead of New York.'"

However, Doug didn't take that opportunity to tell her the film was closing in Minneapolis.

"I couldn't," he said. "I didn't have the heart."

After 115 weeks, the words Harold and Maude are finally taken down from The Westgate marquee.

HAROLD and MAUDE after the WESTGATE

ALTHOUGH *HAROLD AND MAUDE* had finally left The Westgate, it continued to pop up at local theaters, while also growing in reputation nationally in the mid-1970s. Which meant Doug Strand could still see the movie, just a little less regularly.

"They brought it back to the Highland Theater in St. Paul," Doug told me. "In fact, I saw it there a lot, too, because when it closed at the Grandview Theater, they moved it to the Highland and ran it for another month or two."

And it just kept popping up at local theaters. At the Varsity Theater in Minneapolis, one employee explained it this way: "They've run it here three times in the last year already and the audience never gets tired of it."

The owner of the St. Clair Theater in St. Paul, after *Harold and Maude* played for five weeks, declared: "It's an upbeat film that gives an injection of hope to people who need it."

And the manager of the Suburban World theater in Minneapolis, said "People just love that movie." He went on to say that the film would have played longer at the theater if the owners hadn't instituted an X-rated only policy.

Apparently, New York moviegoers were saying the film's lines aloud often enough that an ad asking them to be quiet was required. This was never a problem in Minneapolis.

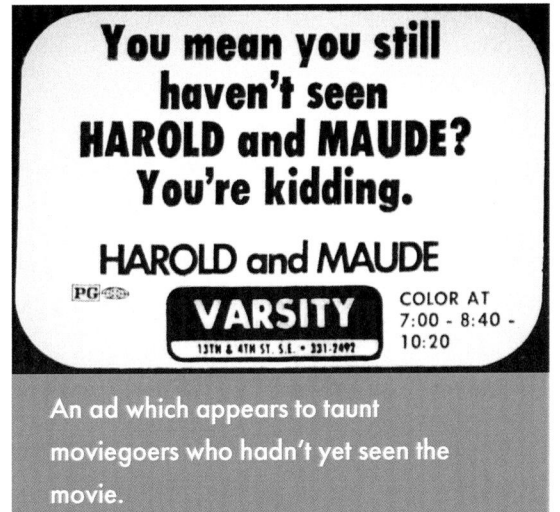

An ad which appears to taunt moviegoers who hadn't yet seen the movie.

But all this wasn't just happening in the Twin Cities. *Harold and Maude* also returned to New York, with an open-ended engagement at the Thalia Theater. Ads for the film read, "What Do They Know in the Midwest That We Don't Know in New York?" and "We've Heard of Word of Mouth, But This Is Ridiculous."

Using the long run in Minneapolis as a key to its advertising, the 300-seat Thalia Theater collected almost $22,000 in tickets for its first week of the film, breaking the 50-year-old theater's box-office record.

Once the film caught on, the theater

The Studio Parnasse theater in Paris (where Harold and Maude ran for a couple of years) as it appears today. It opened in the 1930's and had a 300-seat capacity with orchestra and balcony levels. It was subdivided into smaller auditoriums in 1975 and then later taken over by the MK2 chain.

produced another ad, asking patrons to refrain from reciting the lines along with the film.

And the film just kept going. It played 72 weeks in Detroit, 92 weeks in Boston, and (purportedly) for over two years in Paris from 1972 to 1974 at the Studio Parnasse cinema.

Westgate manager Ralph Watschke was even quoted in *The Montreal Star* about the film and its continued success, when it played in Montreal for 112 weeks.

"Minneapolis is funny," Ralph said. "We have very different tastes. And our theatre is known for playing offbeat films for long times. But *Harold and Maude* I think has something for everyone to relate to. All ages came to see it, although I'd say about 75 percent were under 30."

At the time, Barry London (Paramount's vice president of distribution), said the film's reputation continued to grow, via the college market. "We ship it to college campuses and repertory theaters," he told one reporter. "Most pictures don't mean anything years later, but a new generation of college students is finding this one."

That idea was driven home by an encounter Colin Higgins had with one particular college student.

> What can you say about a two-year-old movie that died... and was reborn largely by word of mouth?
>
> That's "Harold and Maude," the Ruth Gordon and Bud Cort film in which she is 75 and he's 20, and they're a romantic duo. It's been playing to overflow houses these days at the Allston Cinema. The movie has been discovered in waves, first by Middle America, then by teenagers, then by college kids. Three years in Minneapolis, 60 weeks in Detroit. One Doug Strand has seen "Harold and Maude" 138 times so far.
>
> Cult film anyone?

A brief mention in The Boston Globe in June 1974 ... including a shout-out to Doug Strand!

Screenwriter Colin Higgins with Bud Cort and Ruth Gordon.

"A young man came up to me and said, 'Thank you for putting me through college,'" Higgins recounted. "He told me that the first semester of his freshman year at Washington State, he rented the movie and a hall, and made enough to pay his expenses for the semester. He did it again every semester for four years."

"I can walk down the streets of any city," Ruth Gordon explained, "and people hand me oat straw tea. And daisies, daisies, daisies. Two men and two girls brought a floral set-piece of 12 dozen daisies to my hotel in Dayton, Ohio, to show me what it meant to have *Harold and Maude* in Dayton."

Bud Cort had many similar encounters. "Anywhere I've ever gone, James Baldwin, you name it," he said. "People have walked up and said, 'I have to talk to you about this movie.' It's a nice way to meet people."

And then, in the early 1980s, perhaps the biggest surprise of all: The film finally turned a profit.

When Ruth Gordon received her first profit check for the movie (for $50,000), she almost threw the check away. "I thought it was one of

The continued interest in the film led to a re-release from Paramount, with an all-new ad campaign which leaned into the comic suicides and the overall "zaniness" of the film.

Colin Higgins and director Jean-Louis Barrault.

those sweepstakes from the *Reader's Digest*," she said.

For his part, Colin Higgins thought the checks should have been sent out years earlier. "Around 1977," he recalled, "Hal and Ruth and I did an audit of the movie, because it cost so little, we were sure it must be in profit. It wasn't."

Higgins did, however, see some success with his stage play version of the movie, which ran in Paris for years, directed by Jean-Louis Barrault and starring Madeline Renault as Maude.

The Paris version was very well reviewed, with the critic from *Le Monde* Louis Dandrel, placing most of the success of the play on its star, Madeleine Renaud. He kicked off his review by referring to one line in the play: "I too have my secret weapon: my tenderness."

"Which theater line could be more suitable for Madeleine Renaud?" Dandrel wrote. "Her tenderness is not secret, she is only modest. She emerges in every word, in every gesture, she rejuvenates, she beautifies the old lady of *Harold and Maude*, she illuminates her with an inner flame that transfigures her."

"I took my producers when we were in Paris to see it," Higgins recalled. "They don't understand French, and they had tears in their eyes at the end of the play. It's really amazing."

Higgins was also able to visit other productions: Germany, Japan, Canada. "Each time it's different," he explained. "And that's sort of nice to be able to have it as a play, to see it being done differently."

The play went on to be produced around the world (Iceland, Turkey and Brazil) and even closer to home, in a production starring Ellen Geer (Sunshine Doré).

"I got to play Maude, and my daughter played Sunshine Doré," Ellen Geer recalled. "It was like passing it on to a new generation.

Harold and Maude after the Westgate

Madeleine Renaud as Maude and Daniel Rivière as Harold in Jean-Louis Barrault's Paris production of Harold and Maude.

"A young man came up to me afterwards and was sobbing because he said he understood himself better after seeing this play, which was lovely. I was surprised that so many people loved it so much. People still come up and tell me how important it was to them."

The one place the play didn't speak to audiences was the short run it had on Broadway, with Janet Gaynor as Maude. Walter Kerr's review in The New York Times certainly didn't help.

"In some remarkable way, Janet Gaynor has been able to preserve her sweetness down the years, all 73 of them," Kerr wrote. "You like her. You feel protective about her. You want to take her by the hand and get her out of all this. All this being Harold and Maude, the latest version of a relentlessly fey conceit by Colin Higgins that has already done duty as a film, a novel, and a Parisian play. I have not seen any of its earlier incarnations. I have a feeling I've seen the last, though."

He ended his review with this: "Before leaving her young swain, Maude reassures him, 'And this, too, shall pass.' Promise?"

librettist Tom Jones (*The Fantasticks*) and scoring partner Joseph Thalken.

Charles Isherwood, critic for *The New York Times*, was not impressed.

"It's impossible, unfortunately," he wrote, "to resist replaying the charms of the movie in your mind as you watch Tom Jones and Joseph Thalken's tepid stage adaptation, in a wan production enlivened by the brisk presence of Estelle Parsons as Maude. Anyone with a pronounced affection for the movie is likely to leave wishing that one of the most appealing

Ellen Geer (Sunshine Doré in the movie) as Maude and Aaron Angello as Harold in the Will Geer's Theatricum Botanicum production of the play.

A revival of the play thirty-eight years later didn't fare much better, with *The New York Times* critic saying, "The play, like the film before it, feels like one elongated life lesson, this time minus the Cat Stevens songs."

For many people, the songs of Cat Stevens/Yusuf had made the original movie feel like a musical. So perhaps it wasn't too much of a leap to think the core story would make an engaging original stage musical as well.

The result was *Harold and Maude: An Intimate Musical*, created by veteran

Harold and Maude after the Westgate

Actors Janet Gaynor & Keith McDermott in a scene from the Broadway production of Harold & Maude.

couples in movie history had been left to rest in peace, as they most certainly would have preferred."

The critic at *Variety* seemed to agree, writing that "the subtlety and socially conscious whimsy of director Hal Ashby and screenwriter Colin Higgins' delicate flower of a movie is largely lost in the necessarily broader strokes of a staged musical."

The music of the film, of course, had always been one of its strongest attributes. Even back during its original release, the folks at Paramount understood the power of the songs. Studio exec Robert Evans put it this way: "The whole thing rested, quite frankly, on the music. Take the music out … you can't release it."

And his counterpart at the studio, Peter Bart, agreed: "It's the music. Boy does that live on, doesn't it?"

#

Estelle Parsons and Eric Millegan in the musical version of Harold and Maude.

While the music lived on, it was years and years (and years) before fans had anything resembling a complete soundtrack album for the film.

"I refused to allow them to make a soundtrack album," Yusuf explained, "because they were using so much of my two albums – *Mona Bone Jakon* and *Tea for the Tillerman*

Actors (L-R) Keith McDermott, Ruth Ford & Berit Lagerwall in a scene from the Broadway play Harold & Maude.

Harold and Maude after the Westgate

For years, you could get most (but not all) of the songs from the movie from these two albums.

– that it was ending up to be a Greatest Hits. And I (was) too young to have a Greatest Hits. So that was kept out of the contract."

Much of Yusuf's concern was the fact that Ashby had – essentially – used demo versions of the two original songs (*Don't Be Shy* and *If You Want To Sing Out*) in the film.

"I was kind of a little bit upset about that," Yusuf said at the time, "because I wanted to do the songs properly. The songs they finally used were the original demos, rough pieces of work which I meant to finish. It came out and everybody wanted to have the soundtrack. I said, 'No way,' because I never finished those songs."

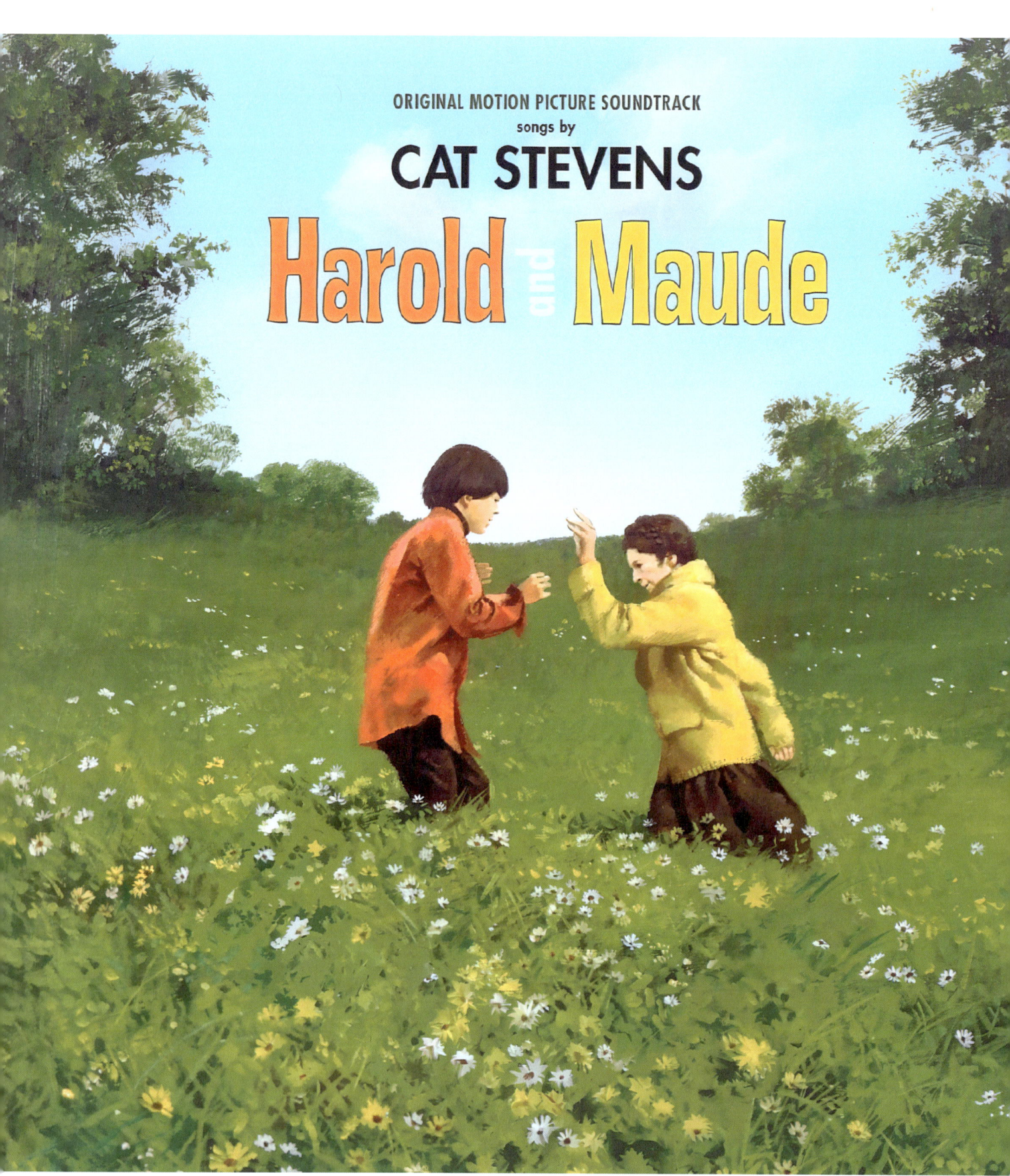

Harold and Maude after the Westgate

Finally! Two options for soundtrack enthusiasts.

Yusuf finally relented, releasing one version of the soundtrack in 2007 and another in 2022 (this one including snippets of dialogue from the film), giving fans the albums they'd been longing for – a mere 35 (and 50) years after the film's release.

Like the music, the power of *Harold and Maude* lives on.

"If I'd never gotten a profit check, it would have been worth it," Ruth Gordon declared back in 1983. "People stop me in the street. In Paris, they say, 'C'est Maude!' Yesterday I was leaving the house when the tour bus came to the end of my street. 'And there she is!' the people on the bus shouted.

"And they started to applaud."

Ruth would be delighted to know that audiences are still applauding to this day.

The WESTGATE after HAROLD and MAUDE

The next HAROLD and MAUDE?

IRVING BERLIN PURPORTEDLY ONCE quipped, "The toughest thing about being a success is that you have to keep being a success."

That was the biggest problem facing General Cinema and their film booker for The Westgate Theater: how to follow-up *Harold and Maude* with something which (hopefully) might generate equal public interest?

As assistant manager Randy Greene remembered, "Yeah, they tried. They brought in a foreign film called *The Tall Blond Man With One Black Shoe*. It was supposed to be a quirky comedy kind of thing. It didn't do that well."

Noting that the proposed replacement had developed a cult following in other parts of the country, *Minneapolis Tribune* columnist Will Jones provided his own take on the company's conundrum:

"With *Harold and Maude* finally running out of its highly specialized kind of box-office gas early in its third year at The Westgate Theater," Jones wrote, "the choice of General Cinema for a successor is *The Tall Blond Man with One Black Shoe*. The commercially successful cult film is a strange bird, and nobody can predict its reception in a given area. The theater folk are always hoping to find one, however, and when they think they sniff a winner, they back it with heavy advertising for a few weeks to give it a chance to find its audience."

Minneapolis Tribune critic Bob Lundegaard shared that view: "Like *Harold and Maude*, which preceded it at The Westgate theater," he wrote, "*The Tall Blond Man With One Black Shoe* is an offbeat comedy that failed to survive the hit-or-miss rigors of downtown bookings and is being given a second life in the suburbs. Will it be another *Harold and Maude*? Will the star, Pierre Richard, fly over from France to cut the birthday cake for the

The Westgate ran a number of preview screenings of *The Tall Blond Man...*, hoping to build an audience before the film officially started.

Much of the film's advertising focused on Mireille Darc's backless dress, which would make another appearance at The Westgate a few years later with Julie Christie in Shampoo.

second anniversary? Will the Westgate's neighbors picket the theater in 1976 and demand a change in fare? Frankly, I doubt it."

Nationally, critics were split on the film. Roger Ebert's view was that "the premise is good, and there are a bunch of good laughs in the movie, but in the end it's not really a superior comedy. It's too slack for my taste."

Opinions were more positive over at *The New York Times*. Vincent Canby declared the film "isn't a comedy of the highest order, but most of it is thoroughly winning," while J. Hoberman offered that the film is "briskly paced and exceedingly droll."

Did Westgate audiences agree? Up to a point: The film ran for more weeks than *How To Murder a Rich Uncle* but fewer than *The Twelve Chairs*.

While the theater returned to operating as a traditional second or third-run house, management kept experimenting with features they hoped might generate a *Harold and Maude*-type repeat-viewing juggernaut.

Amid bookings of traditional studio fare (such as *The Godfather*, *Daisy Miller* and *The Parallax View*), four films were offered as possible successors to the legacy of *Harold and Maude*.

The first big contender was *S*P*Y*S*. From a marketing perspective, the re-teaming of Donald Sutherland and Elliot Gould after *M*A*S*H* seemed like a no-brainer. Sort of a Hope and Crosby for the 1970s.

The reality, however, proved to be more analogous to that ill-fated sequel to the *M*A*S*H* television series, *After M*A*S*H*, which ranks – with *Joanie Loves Chachi* and *Joey* – as one of the worst spin-offs of all time.

And critics agreed. The headline for *The New York Times* review of *S*P*Y*S* read: "Sutherland and Gould Attempt C.I.A. Spoof." The reviewer, Nora Sayre, went on to write: "The only mystery contained in *S*P*Y*S*, a feeble attempt to spoof the

The re-pairing of Donald Sutherland and Elliot Gould (along with the asterisks from M*A*S*H) made a comic promise which the film failed to keep.

The Mad Magazine-style artwork for the Bank Shot poster screamed "zany."

Central Intelligence Agency, is why Donald Sutherland and Elliott Gould ever chose to be in it."

Leonard Maltin was less verbose but equally biting, rating the film a bomb, laughless, and "unworthy of anyone's time."

S*P*Y*S lasted for two weeks at The Westgate, before being replaced by the next long-run contender, *Bank Shot*.

Bank Shot had an interesting if eclectic pedigree: based on a novel by Donald Westlake – and directed by eight-time Tony award winner Gower Champion – it's a sort of sequel to *The Hot Rock*, with George C. Scott playing the Robert Redford role.

Bank Shot co-starred Harold's psychiatrist (G. Wood) and one of the actors who read for the part of Harold (Bob Balaban). Despite those interesting ingredients, it wasn't the right recipe for a new *Harold and Maude*.

Local critic Bob Lundegaard put it this way: "The Westgate Theater, which struck gold a while back with its two-year run of *Harold and Maude,* is trying for a second strike with its current production, *Bank Shot*. Like *Harold and Maude, Bank Shot* had a short run downtown and seemed destined for oblivion, despite the fact that it stars George C. Scott.

Bank Shot performer Bob Balaban (right) was one of six actors who screen-tested for Harold in Harold and Maude.

The Westgate after Harold and Maude

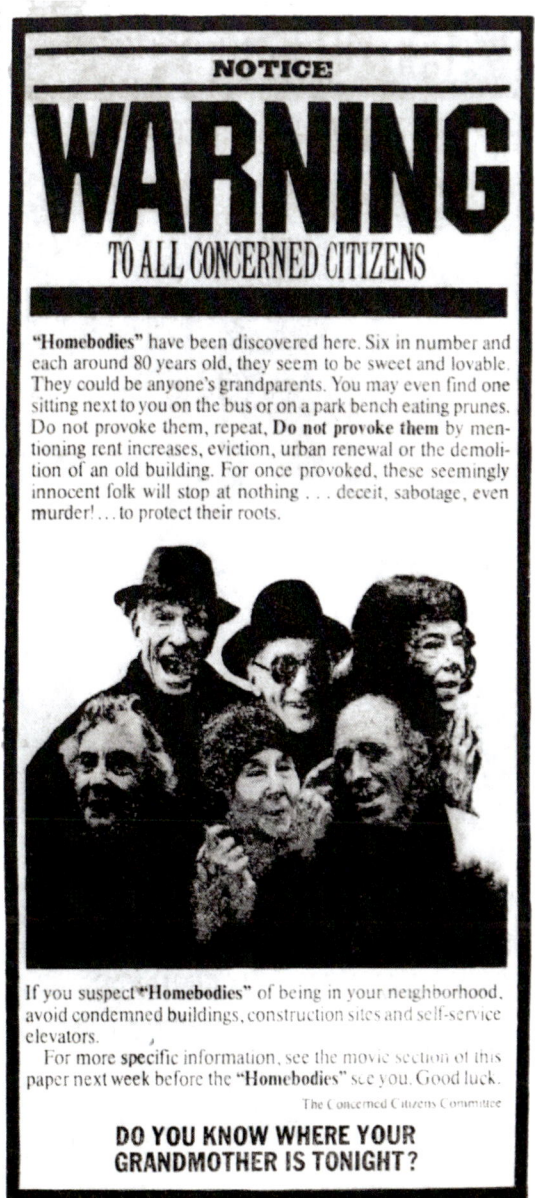

When is a movie ad not a movie ad? When it never mentions the name of the movie, the theater where it's playing, or the fact that it's a movie.

"Some of the bosses at General Cinema, however, apparently feel it has the same kind of offbeat humor that *Harold and Maude* had, and they're holding it over for another week, despite middling crowds. I caught up with it over the weekend at The Westgate, and I'm sorry to say that even with all those good intentions, a *Harold and Maude* it's not."

Audiences agreed. The film played for three weeks before being pulled.

More traditional movies were booked for the next month, before they tried to woo audiences with another offbeat film, *Homebodies*. They matched the quirky nature of the film – senior citizens knocking off people who want to tear down their apartment flat – with an equally wacky ad campaign.

Based around the tagline "Do You Know Where Your Grandmother Is Tonight?" the ad was positioned as a public health campaign without any mention of the movie itself.

Local critic Don Morrison's review headline summed up the general critical consensus about the film: "Sometimes Killing Isn't Humorous."

He went on to write: "I attended *Homebodies* in anticipation of a spot of macabre humor to cheer an otherwise wintry Sunday afternoon. I came away pondering the semantic differences between 'macabre' and 'morbid.'

"The newspaper and television ads for *Homebodies* yuk the movie up as if it were a comedy, one of those familiar, chucklesome items in which murder doesn't count because the murderers are cute and quaint (in this case, pruney-looking senior citizens).

"The situation of the initial 'harmless' murder isn't even remotely amusing and, after things get wholly grim, absurd or ludicrous bits of business are dropped into the muddled stew to ruin any saving note of reality. The sad conclusion is that *Homebodies* has no point of view whatever – comic or otherwise – and ultimately exposes itself as merely a slick idea damaged in handling."

Homebodies succumbed to an early passing at The Westgate; it only lasted two weeks, before being replaced with a not-so-inspired *Harold and Maude* and *Where's Poppa?* double-feature.

After that, management tried one last time to find a true successor to *Harold and Maude*. And, as they say, sometimes fourth time's the charm.

The Westgate after Harold and Maude

KING of HEARTS

With *King of Hearts*, General Cinema was finally able to find a movie for The Westgate with a positive outlook on life similar to *Harold and Maude* … while also sharing the long-running film's outsider point of view, plus its warmth and wit.

Originally released in 1967, *King of Hearts* is an anti-war comedy-drama set during World War I, about a Scottish soldier who is sent to disarm a bomb in a French town evacuated by its residents but taken over by asylum inmates. When the inmates escape and assume the roles of the townspeople, the soldier finds their peaceful, loving community preferable to the insanity of war, ultimately choosing to remain with them rather than return to the battlefield.

Minneapolis Tribune critic Bob Lundegaard immediately recognized the potential with this film.

"The people who live near the Westgate Theater in Edina may be dusting off their

Alan Bates wears a kilt in this promotional shot for King of Hearts. He wears far less in the film's poster.

picket signs one of these years," he wrote in his review. "The variety-craving neighbors, you'll recall, got indignant when The Westgate played *Harold and Maude* for more than two years.

"Well, The Westgate may have another *Harold and Maude* on its hands, if theater manager Ralph Watschke is any judge. He's been showing the 1967 French comedy *King of Hearts* for five weeks, and so far the size and enthusiasm of the crowds – especially the packed houses on weekends – remind him of the initial response to *Harold and Maude*.

"One customer claims to have seen it 18 times. I can't match that record and have no intention of trying. But I did zip over to The Westgate on two occasions in the past two weeks – the second time to see if the film was really worth a second look. I don't think it is, but it's definitely worth a first look. It has a hilarious premise – an evacuated French town in World War I is abandoned to the inmates of the town's insane asylum – and a fine cast of French character actors play the lunatics."

Vincent Canby in *The New York Times* agreed, calling the film an "extravagant and highly comic morality play," declaring the film to be "a funny and touching experience."

King of Hearts settled in for a comfortable six month run at The Westgate.

Meanwhile, the next big drama for the theater would actually take place off screen.

The Westgate after Harold and Maude

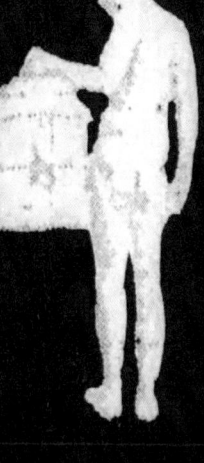

The King's Loyal Short Subjects: Bambi Meets Godzilla & Thank You Mask Man

    Just as *Harold and Maude* was accompanied by the wildly popular short, *De Düva*, *King of Hearts* also came with what came to be called his loyal short subjects: *Bambi Meets Godzilla* and *Thank You Mask Man*. This shorts duo had been paired with the feature for years, and so it made sense to continue that tradition during its Westgate run.

    Marv Newland created *Bambi Meets Godzilla* as a student film in 1969. Its 91-second running time consists of 50 seconds of opening credits and 29 seconds for the closing credits. That left 12 seconds for the short action that brings the title to life.

Newland recalled the genesis of the film: "*Bambi Meets Godzilla* was based on my joke: 'Do you want to hear the soundtrack to the world's shortest movie?' I then gave a high-pitched squeal of fear, followed by a low-pitched, deep roar/growl. The recipient would ask something like, 'What's that?' I would say, '*Bambi Meets Godzilla*.'"

The animation consists of about 50 rough drawings; Newland often joked that it took more time to shoot the film than it did to draw it.

The short, which is still popular today, had a bigger impact on comedy culture than you might imagine, acting as the inspiration for the conclusion of one of the best-known opening credits sequences of all time.

"Terry Gilliam took me out for lunch in London years ago," Newland explained, "and confessed to having lifted this foot stomp gag from *Bambi Meets Godzilla* for the *Monty Python* animation."

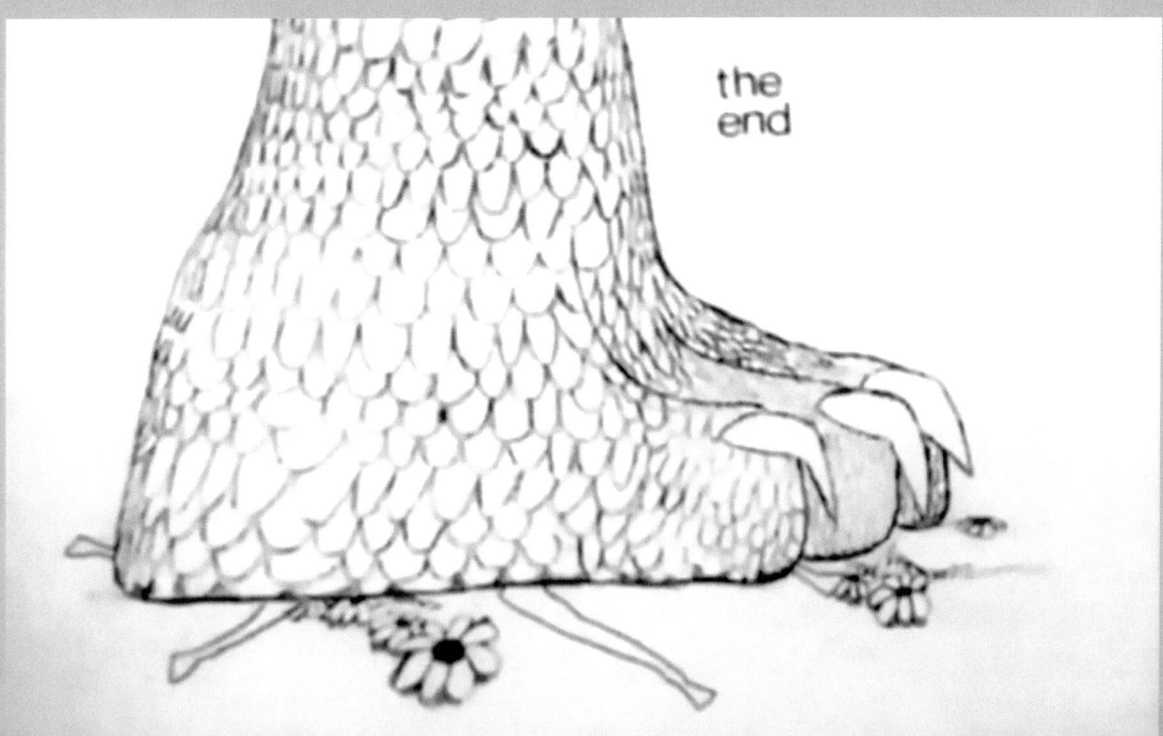

Thank You Mask Man got its start as a seriously NSFW routine by Lenny Bruce, in which he took the Lone Ranger mythos apart in a funny and profane sketch, during which Bruce enacted all the various roles (such as The Lone Ranger, assorted Townspeople and an uncommonly thankful youngster).

The routine was one of several cited in the *People vs. Bruce* obscenity trial, where the comedian claimed what the prosecution called obscene was simple incongruity employed for comic effect. The jury

deadlocked on the question and a mistrial was declared by the judge.

Artist Jeff Hale (who later went on to animate the well-known *Pinball Number Countdown* on *Sesame Street*, as well as several popular characters for the show), created the animation in 1968, two years after Lenny Bruce's death.

The film was originally scheduled to debut on the opening night of the San Francisco International Film Festival but was unexpectedly pulled from the program. When it was eventually released, it faced significant controversy, prompting many theaters to refuse to show it. This initial backlash, combined with an unprofitable run, made for a difficult start.

However, the film gained a dedicated following over time, particularly after being broadcast multiple times on the USA Network's *Night Flight*. Its growing popularity eventually cemented its cult status, with Landmark Theaters regularly screening it as a pre-movie feature for several years.

MEET the NEW BOSS

At the same time the brain trust at General Cinema was trying to find a successful successor to *King of Hearts*, the company suddenly had to deal with the fallout from a federal lawsuit which had been bouncing around the courts since 1971. The suit had been filed after the company bought all the Mann Theaters in the Twin Cities.

In a press release from the Department of Justice (yes, the DOJ puts out press releases, or at least they did back then), the complaint stated: "This acquisition gave General Cinema control of more than 35 percent of all indoor motion picture theaters in the Minneapolis-St. Paul metropolitan area. The Government seeks to have the acquisitions declared illegal and to obtain an order requiring General Cinema to divest itself of all of the acquired theaters."

Department of Justice

FOR IMMEDIATE RELEASE
MONDAY, SEPTEMBER 13, 1971

The Department of Justice filed a civil antitrust suit today seeking to have General Cinema Corporation of Boston, Massachusetts divest itself of 21 indoor motion picture theatres it acquired in the Minneapolis-St. Paul metropolitan area in 1970 and 1971.

Attorney General John N. Mitchell said the suit was filed in United States District Court in Minneapolis, Minnesota.

The complaint charged that General Cinema's acquisition of substantially all of the assets of Mann Theatres in August 1970, and its acquisition of the State Theatre in January 1971, violated Section 7 of the Clayton Act by increasing concentration and eliminating actual and potential competition in the bidding for feature motion pictures in the Minneapolis-St. Paul area.

The complaint also charged that, as a result of the acquistions, General Cinema's bargaining power with motion picture distributors has been enhanced to the detriment of the smaller theatre circuits and individual theatres with which it competes for licenses to exhibit feature motion pictures.

Anti-Trust paperwork from the Department of Justice, back when the Attorney General was a guy named John Mitchell.

The Westgate after Harold and Maude

- 2 -

Assistant Attorney General Richard W. McLaren, in charge of the Antitrust Division, said that General Cinema, with approximately 246 theatres as of November 1970, operates one of the largest motion picture theatre circuits in the United States.

He also stated that Mann Theatres, with a chain of approximately 20 indoor theatres in the Minneapolis-St. Paul metropolitan area, was the largest motion picture exhibitor in the area at the time it was acquired by General Cinema.

According to the complaint, General Cinema operated two indoor motion picture theatres in the Minneapolis-St. Paul metropolitan area prior to its acquisition of Mann Theatres.

That acquisition, together with its acquisition of the State Theatre, the second largest indoor motion picture theatre in the area, gave General Cinema control of more than 35 percent of all indoor motion picture theatres in the Minneapolis-St. Paul metropolitan area, the complaint said.

The Government seeks to have the acquisitions declared illegal and to obtain an order requiring General Cinema to divest itself of all of the acquired theatres.

In purchasing those twenty-one theaters, General Cinema was charged with violating Section 7 of the Clayton Act by "increasing concentration and eliminating actual and potential competition in the bidding for feature motion pictures in the Minneapolis-St Paul area."

One of the ways General Cinema met the conditions of the settlement, was to immediately sublease nine of its theaters (including The Westgate) to the Metropolitan Theater Company, run by a plumbing and heating contractor from Stillwater, Ernest Peaslee, Jr.

Peaslee had been in the movie theater business since 1959, operating theaters in Minnesota, Wisconsin and North Dakota. He and the company got off to a quick start in Minneapolis, offering an odd array of second-run and third-run films (plus some X-rated options).

They also instituted a weekly program of children's matinees, including cartoons, comedies and that much beloved children's classic, *The Andromeda Strain*.

After acquiring nine theaters from General Cinema, Metropolitan hit the ground running, presenting a Walking Tall take-off, an X-rated film called Happy Days (no relation to the sitcom of the same name) and a second-run of a Kurt Russell/Disney film.

They even brought back *Harold and Maude* (twice!) and briefly presented the bizarre reissue of *Where's Poppa?*, which for some reason had been re-released under the hilarious new title, *Going Ape*.

The only change made to Where's Poppa? when it became Going Ape was a clumsy edit during the opening titles, when the old name was pulled out and the new one jammed in.

Metropolitan was all about promotions, which they called their "Cavalcade of Entertainment," including live shows with the casts of American Graffiti and the Our Gang films.

Despite their best efforts, in just five months the Metropolitan Theater Company had run out of the steam (and operating capital) needed to run The Westgate and the eight other theaters. At which point, General Cinema stepped back into the picture …

... SAME as the OLD BOSS

THE WESTGATE CLOSED IN early October 1975 but was quickly re-opened (along with the other theaters) by General Cinema less than a month later.

As reported in a brief article in *The Star Tribune*, "A General Cinema executive said in a telephone interview from Boston, the company's headquarters, that the company is 'still obligated to sell the theaters under the court order, and we're still looking for a purchaser who will satisfy the federal court.' Meanwhile, General Cinema will reopen the theaters because it has mortgage or rental payments of its own on the properties, the executive said.

"He said that General Cinema would continue operating the theaters and that 'it's now up to the court to tell us what to do. The court knows we are taking them back. I'm going to assume that if someone else comes along and wants to lease them from us, we'll lease them.'"

The issue went back to the courts and General Cinema once again began booking films into The Westgate Theater ...

The Westgate's cinematic offering to moviegoers in September, 1974 (complete with the misspelling of the star's name on the marquee).

THIS is THE END

... BUT THEY STILL couldn't quite figure out how to make the small theater profitable.

Upon taking the theater back from Metropolitan, General Cinema offered the traditional string of second-and third-run movies: *Mahogany, Shampoo, Billy Jack*.

But from time to time, they tossed in an occasional 'quirky' film, clearly hoping to rekindle the *Harold and Maude* magic: *The Apprenticeship of Duddy Kravitz, 92 In The Shade, The Return of the Tall Blond Man with One Black Shoe*.

One real long shot was *Mr. Sycamore*. Based on a 1942 play, it's about a mild-mannered mailman (Jason Robards) who dreams of turning himself into a tree – a sycamore. Although it re-teamed Robards with Sandy Dennis (the pair had performed together in *A Thousand Clowns* on Broadway), the film never really took root. It lasted two weeks and was chopped down in favor of a rebooking of *King of Hearts*.

General Cinema later took another big swing with *Jackson County Jail*, positioning the film in their advertisements as (oddly) a potential successor to *Harold and Maude*:

Over the years, The Westgate Theatre

In Mr. Sycamore, Jason Robards wants to turn into a tree. Spoiler alert: He gets his wish, which does little more than annoy Sandy Dennis.

has presented many unique films previously overlooked by the public and, as a result, has created a new appreciation of many outstanding works.

Any movie which was vaguely "quirky" got sent to The Westgate, including an unneeded sequel to an earlier French quasi-hit.

Now, we are offering a film which, while successful on an exploitive level, has much more to offer to the discriminating film viewer. Vincent Canby said of it, "The surprise movie of the summer. Filmmaking of relentless energy and harrowing excitement" and Gene Shalit added, "Explosive – An unpretentious action drama made with a tough intelligence."

We might add that Jackson County Jail is crisp, chilling, shocking, honest and immensely exciting. A true sleeper which Twin City audiences may make, in its own way, as phenomenal as Harold and Maude. Be one of the first to see Yvette Mimieux in Jackson County Jail.

Although the ad quoted Canby's positive review, it did leave out the final caveat he had offered: "I hesitate to say too much, thus oversell a movie that is best come upon without great expectations."

Leonard Maltin seemed to agree, saying the film was "livelier than most," but only giving the film two-and-a-half stars.

When *Jackson County Jail* failed to serve is full sentence (it lasted about three weeks), The Westgate turned to a series of odd double features (*Silent Running* paired with *Minnie & Moskowitz*; *Obsession* teamed with *Monty Python and the Holy Grail*; *Guess Who's Coming To Dinner* bundled with *The Mouse That Roared*).

After that, it drifted into becoming a quasi-revival house, a popular format where old movie double-features were paired up for three days or a week at a time (*The Maltese Falcon & The Petrified Forrest, Holiday & The Awful Truth, Casablanca & Now Voyager*).

And then came the news that The Westgate – along with three other General Cinema theaters – was shutting down.

On July 8, 1977, *The Star Tribune* reported that "The General Cinema Corp. will close four area movie theaters next Thursday. The apparent reason for the closings is low profits. The four theaters were among eight that General Cinema closed for a month in 1975 because the operator to whom it had leased the theaters was behind in his rent.

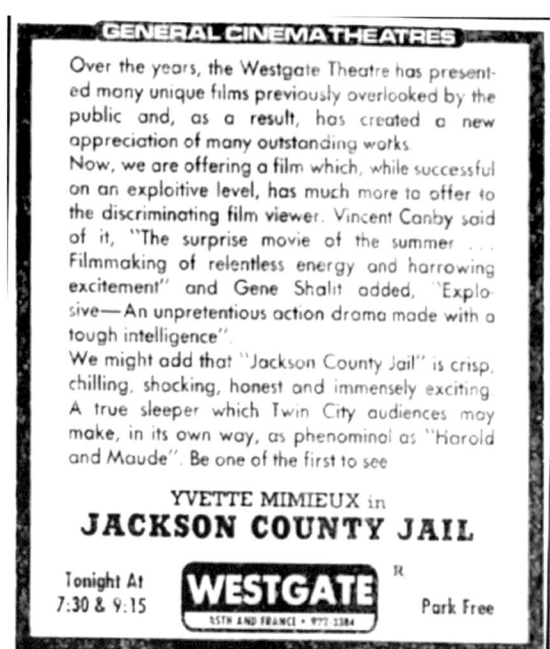

The Westgate after Harold and Maude

The struggle to find a film as popular as Harold and Maude led the folks at General Cinema down an odd array of cinematic dead ends.

"It reopened them because it was under a federal court order to operate them until a suitable buyer could be found. It was unclear yesterday whether General Cinema had obtained court permission for the latest closings."

Although the articles said the movie houses were being shut down immediately, The Westgate hung on for a couple more months before finally closing its doors in early September 1977.

The Westgate's final feature film offering was *The Late Show*, a truly under-rated gem starring Art Carney and Lily Tomlin, written and directed by Robert Benton.

Leonard Maltin, giving the film three and-a-half stars, reviewed it this way: "Carney is an aging private eye who tries to solve the murder of his ex-partner, 'helped' by a flaky, aimless young woman (Tomlin). Echoes of

> 2 Entertaining Hits!
> "SILENT RUNNING" | "MINNIE MOSKOWITZ"
> AT 7:00 & 10:25 — WESTGATE — AT 8:30
> 45TH AND FRANCE • 922-3384   PG

Chandler and Hammett resound in Benton's complex but likable script; chemistry between Carney and Tomlin is perfect."

Pauline Kael agreed, saying "Benton's nostalgia for the genre works imaginatively in every detail of the film. This one-of-a-kind murder

Toward the end, some of the film pairings at The Westgate seemed not only random, but desperately random. And the ads got a little sloppy as well, such as leaving the ampersand out of Minnie & Moskowitz.

> RETROSPECTIVES
> "Guess Who's Coming To Dinner?" Tonight at 7:30 Tom. At 1:00-4:20-7:40
> — PLUS —
> "The Mouse That Roared" Tonight 9:25 • Tom. 2:50-6:10-9:30
> WESTGATE   G
> 45TH AND FRANCE • 922-3384

The Westgate after Harold and Maude

mystery pays off in atmosphere, spooking us by the flip, greedy ordinariness of evil."

With the final screening of *The Late Show* – and just two months short of its forty-second birthday – The Westgate Theater's curtains came to a close and the marquee lights were shut off for the final time.

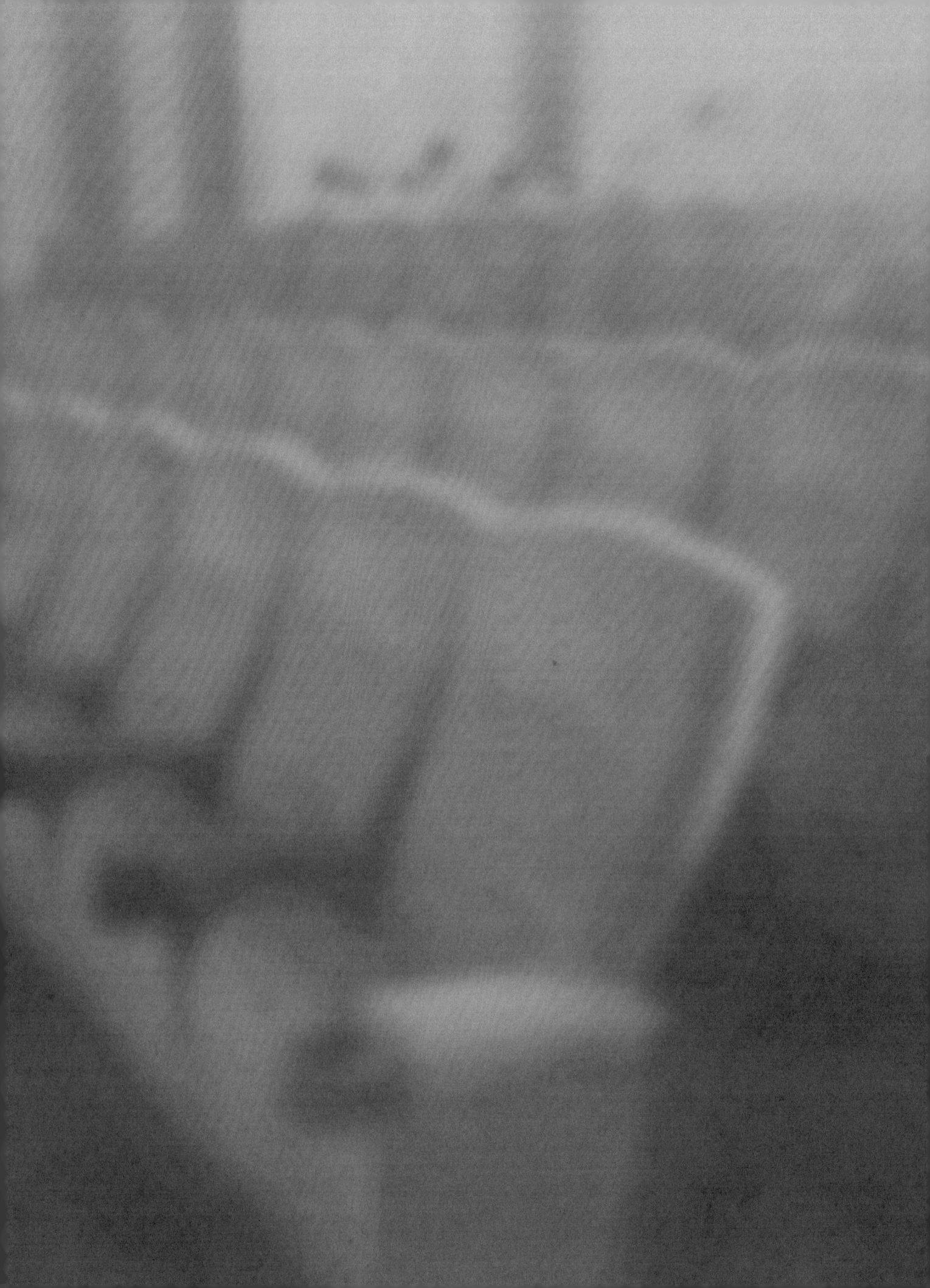

CODA

Although the interior has been completely overhauled, the exterior of The Edina Theater is pretty much still the same. It's one of eight movie theaters in Minnesota still owned by The Mann Theater organization.

THE STORY OF THE Westgate Theater is similar to that of most neighborhood theaters in the 1970s as they struggled to survive amid changing movie-viewing habits and the introduction of multiplex theaters.

The Westgate's unique difference, of course, was its relationship with *Harold and Maude*, which did a pretty good job of cementing the theater's reputation in cinema history.

Of the three neighborhood theaters I frequented in my teens, only one survives: The Edina Theater, which has been completely redesigned as a four-screen multiplex.

For a while, The Boulevard was split (badly) into two auditoriums, offering the unique sensation of simultaneously seeing one movie while hearing two. And then it went away entirely, replaced first by (ironically) a video store, and then (unironically) a math tutoring center.

The Westgate, however, has completely disappeared.

For several years it was taken over by the industrial laundry next door; the marquee was removed, the library and the beauty salon were gone, and all traces of Carl Fust's vision were erased.

Today, even the large industrial laundry is gone. In its place is The Lorient, a luxury complex, offering 45 apartments, a rooftop terrace, underground parking and – get this – a Club Room, suitable for meetings and small social events. A Club Room! The one holdover amenity from Carl Fust's original plan for the space has once again returned!

Harold and Maude is still with us, though, in frequent revivals, screenings on Turner Classic Movies, and an extra-filled Blu-Ray from The Criterion Collection.

The overhead garage door to the public parking ramp in the middle of The Lorient building is pretty much exactly where the box office was located, back when this was The Westgate Theater.

The transformation from gala showplace to neighborhood eyesore is complete. This is how the building looked when it became part of an industrial laundry.

The exterior of what was once The Boulevard Theater. The bright marquee lights seem to suggest a level of excitement heretofore unheard of in traditional math tutoring.

Or, if you've got the travel bug, you can fly over to the tiny (44 seat) Galerie Cinema in Essen, Germany, which has shown *Harold and Maude* every Sunday since 1975.

Paramount executive Peter Bart might have explained the film's legacy best when he said, "In its own small way, *Harold and Maude* – this odd little movie about death – achieved its own immortality."

However, my final sentiments align with those of Ralph Watschke, the long-time Westgate Theater manager, who after the film ran 1,957 times at his theater, summed up his feelings about the movie this way:

"I'm looking forward to seeing it again."

Me too, Ralph. Me too.

ABOUT the AUTHOR

Although John hasn't seen *Harold and Maude* as many times as Doug Strand, he's certainly seen it more than most people.

His short documentary about Ruth and Bud's 1974 visit to Minneapolis (*The Twin Cities Welcomes Ruth Gordon and Bud Cort*) can easily be found on YouTube. And links to his other longer films can be found at his film site, www.fastcheapfilm.com/

In addition to his popular filmmaking books (*Fast, Cheap and Under Control* and *Fast, Cheap and Written That Way*), John is also the author of the Eli Marks mystery series and the Como Lake Players mystery series. Plus, he's written four greyhound-themed pastiches.

You can learn more at AlbertsBridgeBooks.com.

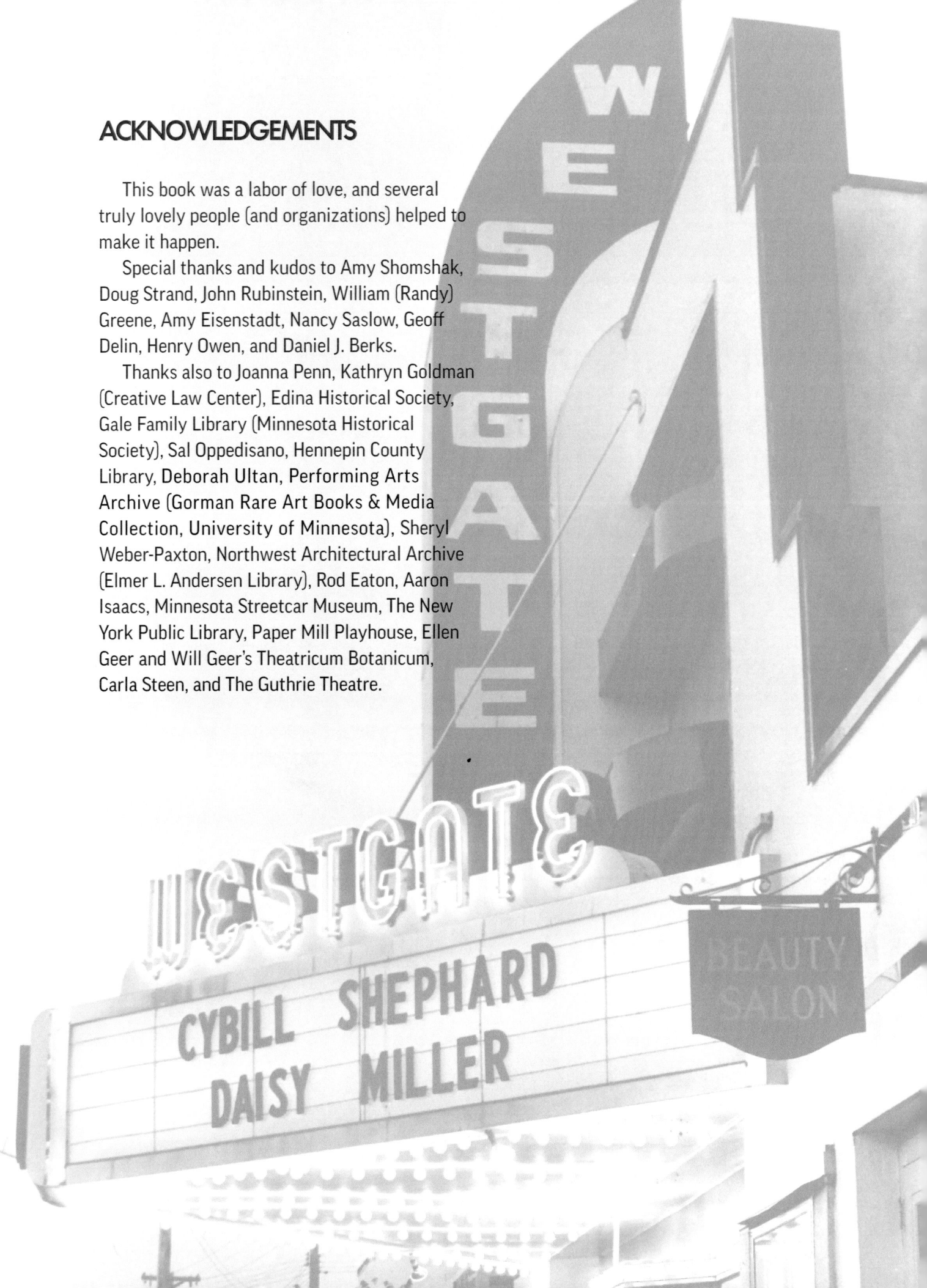

ACKNOWLEDGEMENTS

This book was a labor of love, and several truly lovely people (and organizations) helped to make it happen.

Special thanks and kudos to Amy Shomshak, Doug Strand, John Rubinstein, William (Randy) Greene, Amy Eisenstadt, Nancy Saslow, Geoff Delin, Henry Owen, and Daniel J. Berks.

Thanks also to Joanna Penn, Kathryn Goldman (Creative Law Center), Edina Historical Society, Gale Family Library (Minnesota Historical Society), Sal Oppedisano, Hennepin County Library, Deborah Ultan, Performing Arts Archive (Gorman Rare Art Books & Media Collection, University of Minnesota), Sheryl Weber-Paxton, Northwest Architectural Archive (Elmer L. Andersen Library), Rod Eaton, Aaron Isaacs, Minnesota Streetcar Museum, The New York Public Library, Paper Mill Playhouse, Ellen Geer and Will Geer's Theatricum Botanicum, Carla Steen, and The Guthrie Theatre.

PHOTO CREDITS

Cover

Westgate Theater Photo, Author Collection.

Introduction

Page 3–4: Westgate, Edina and Boulevard Theaters photos, Author Collection

Page 5: World Theater Photo by Mike Evangelist. Used by permission.

The Westgate Before *Harold and Maude*

Pages 11–23: Westgate Theater and Carl Fust photos, courtesy of the Marjorie Fust Delin family collection. Used by permission.

Page 11: Aerial View France Avenue, courtesy of Minnesota Streetcar Museum. Used by permission.

Page 14: Westgate Exterior Sketch, courtesy of Northwest Architectural Archive. Used by permission.

Page 17: Grand Opening Program, courtesy of the Marjorie Fust Delin family collection. Used by permission.

Page 18: Westgate Exterior Photo, Courtesy Hennepin County Library. Used by permission.

Page 19: Lady Tubbs production stills, courtesy of Alamy Stock Images. Used by permission.

Pages 19–21: Lady Tubbs Poster, Make Believe Revue and Lady In Black images, reproduced in compliance with Fair Use for commentary and education.

Page 20: Meet Nero Wolf Production Still, courtesy of Everett Stock Images. Used by permission.

Page 21: Meet Nero Wolf Lobby Card, courtesy of Everett Stock Images. Used by permission.

Page 24: Tall in the Saddle Poster, courtesy of Alamy Stock Images. Used by permission.

Page 25: Westgate Lobby, Ground Plan, courtesy of Northwest Architectural Archive. Used by permission.

Page 28: Ted Mann article, reproduced in compliance with Fair Use for commentary and education.

Page 29: Tippi Hedren Photo, Edina Historical Society, used by permission.

Page 32: General Cinema Corporation Logo, reproduced in compliance with Fair Use for commentary and education.

Page 34: The Twelve Chairs Poster, courtesy of Alamy Stock Images. Used by permission

Page 35: The Twelve Chairs Production Still, courtesy of Alamy Stock Images. Used by permission.

Page 39: Where's Poppa? (Ruth and George), courtesy of Alamy Stock Images. Used by permission.

Pages 40–41: Where's Poppa? (George, Ruth and Ron), courtesy of Alamy Stock Images. Used by permission.

Harold and Maude Before The Westgate

Page 47: Edward and Mildred Lewis photo, creator and source unknown, reproduced in compliance with Fair Use for commentary and education.

Page 48: Harold and Maude production still, courtesy of Alamy Stock Images. Used by permission.

Page 49: Hal Ashby directs, courtesy of Alamy Stock Images. Used by permission.

Page 50: Ruth Gordon, Rosemary's Baby, courtesy of Alamy Stock Images. Used by permission.

Page 51: John Rubinstein and Elsa Lanchester headshots, courtesy of Alamy Stock Images. Used by permission.

Page 52: Vivian Pickles, courtesy of Everett Stock Images. Used by permission.

Page 53: Shari Summers as Edith Fern, courtesy of MPTV Images. Used by permission.

Page 54: Bud looking down at the camera, courtesy of MPTV Images. Used by permission.

Page 56: Hal and Vivian walk down to pool, courtesy of MPTV Images. Used by permission.

Page 56: Harold, Mother and Sunshine photo, courtesy of Everett Stock Images. Used by permission.

Page 57: Ruth and Bud entering train car, courtesy of MPTV Images. Used by permission.

Page 58: Judy Engels prepped, courtesy of MPTV Images. Used by permission.

Page 59: Hal and Bud with banjo, courtesy of MPTV Images. Used by permission.

Page 61: Ruth and Hal confer on wall, courtesy of MPTV Images. Used by permission.

Page 62: Hal and Ellen on Floor, Bud watches, courtesy of MPTV Images. Used by permission.

Page 63: Harold and Maude with Cop, courtesy of Alamy Stock Images. Used by permission.

Page 63: Hal and Tom confer by car, courtesy of MPTV Images. Used by permission.

Page 66: Ruth, Bud, Hal confer by urban tree, courtesy of MPTV Images. Used by permission.

Page 68: Maude paints the saint, Everett Stock Images. Used by permission.

Page 69: Cat Stevens on Beach, courtesy of Alamy Stock Images. Used by permission.

Page 69: Hal Ashby headshot, courtesy of Alamy Stock Images. Used by permission.

Page 70: French Harold and Maude Poster, courtesy of Alamy Stock Images. Used by permission.

Page 72: Bud and Ruth in greenhouse, courtesy of MPTV Images. Used by permission.

Page 73: Three Harold and Maude posters, Author Collection

Pages 78-81: Harold and Maude production stills, courtesy of Alamy Stock Images. Used by permission.

Harold and Maude at The Westgate

Page 97: Harold Aims at Mother, courtesy of Alamy Stock Images. Used by permission.

Page 98: Harold with Gun, courtesy of Alamy Stock Images. Used by permission.

Page 99: Doug Strand and Ruth Gordon, Shubert Theatre, Boston, shot by Martha Swope on October 1, 1974. From Doug Strand's personal collection. Used by permission.

Page 101: Ruth Interviewed, *Minneapolis Star/ Minneapolis Tribune*, Minnesota Historical Society. Used by permission.

Page 101: Ruth cuts the cake, Minneapolis Star/

Minneapolis Tribune, Minnesota Historical Society. Used by permission.

Page 102: Ruth Gordon in Seventeen, reproduced in compliance with Fair Use for commentary and education.

Page 102: Ruth Gordon in A Dolls House, reproduced in compliance with Fair Use for commentary and education.

Page 103: Ruth Autographs a book, *Minneapolis Star/Minneapolis Tribune*, Minnesota Historical Society. Used by permission.

Page 104: Ruth with Plaque, Minneapolis Star/Minneapolis Tribune, Minnesota Historical Society. Used by permission.

Page 107: Guindon Cartoon, Richard Guindon, *Minneapolis Star,* Minnesota Historical Society. Used by permission.

Page 108: Bud Cort at Dinner, *Minneapolis Star/Minneapolis Tribune,* Minnesota Historical Society. Used by permission.

Page 109: Eric Christmas at The Guthrie, Act One, Too, provided by the Guthrie Theater. Used by permission.

Page 114: Ruth Gordon autographed photo, Author Collection

Page 115: Bud Cort autographed photo, Author Collection

Page 116: Bud and Ruth in front of theater, reproduced in compliance with Fair Use for commentary and education.

Pages 117–118: Protest Photos, *Minneapolis Star/Minneapolis Tribune*, Minnesota Historical Society. Used by permission.

Harold and Maude After The Westgate

Page 128: Parnasse Cinema, Paris. Photo by Amy Shomshak. Used by permission.

Page 129: Colin Higgins with Bud Cort and Ruth Gordon. Courtesy Colin Higgins Trust. Used by permission.

Page 130: *Harold and Maude* Updated Poster, courtesy of Alamy Stock Images. Used by permission.

Page 130: Colin Higgins and Jean-Louis Barrault, reproduced in compliance with Fair Use for commentary and education.

Page 131: Madeleine Renaud and Daniel Rivière in *Harold and Maude,* reproduced in compliance with Fair Use for commentary and education.

Page 132: Ellen Geer in *Harold and Maude,* Will Geer's Theatricum Botanicum. Used by permission.

Pages 133–134: *Harold and Maude* Broadway version. Photos by Martha Swope ©Billy Rose Theatre Division, The New York Public Library for the Performing Arts. Used by permission.

Page 134: Estelle Parsons and Eric Millegan in *Harold & Maude The Musical* (2005) (C) Jerry Dalia, courtesy of the Paper Mill Playhouse. Used by permission.

Page 135: Cat Stevens Album Cover (*Mona Bone Jakon and Tea For The Tillerman*), reproduced in compliance with Fair Use for commentary and education.

Page 136: Harold and Maude Soundtrack Album Cover (2007), reproduced in compliance with Fair Use for commentary and education.

Page 137: Harold and Maude Soundtrack Album Cover (2022), reproduced in compliance with Fair Use for commentary and education.

The Westgate After *Harold and Maude*

Page 141: Tall Blond Man Poster, reproduced in compliance with Fair Use for commentary and education.

Page 142: Tall Blond Man photos, courtesy of Everett Stock Images. Used by permission.

Page 143: *SPYS* Poster, courtesy of Everett Stock Images. Used by permission.

Page 143: *SPYS* photo (Gould & Sutherland), courtesy of Alamy Stock Images. Used by permission.

Page 144: *Bank Shot* Poster, courtesy of Everett Stock Images. Used by permission.

Page 144: Bank Shot Production Still, courtesy of Alamy Stock Images. Used by permission.

Page 145: Homebodies Poster, courtesy of Everett Stock Images. Used by permission.

Page 147: King of Hearts Photo, courtesy of Everett Stock Images. Used by permission.

Page 148: King of Hearts Poster, courtesy of Everett Stock Images. Used by permission.

Pages 154–155: GCC Complaint, reproduced in compliance with Fair Use for commentary and education.

Page 156: Going Ape poster, reproduced in compliance with Fair Use for commentary and education.

Page 158: GCC Cinema Logo, reproduced in compliance with Fair Use for commentary and education.

Page 158: Westgate Theater photo, Author Collection

Page 159: Mr. Sycamore Poster, reproduced in compliance with Fair Use for commentary and education.

Page 160: *Jackson County Jail* Production Still, courtesy of Alamy Stock Images. Used by permission.

Page 161: Duddy Kravitz Poster, 92 In the Shade Poster, and Jackson County Jail Poster courtesy of Alamy Stock Images. Used by permission.

Page 163: *The Late Show* Poster, courtesy of Alamy Stock Images. Used by permission.

Page 163: *The Late Show* Production Still, courtesy of Alamy Stock Images. Used by permission.

Coda

Page 167: Edina Theater today, Author Collection.

Page 168: The Lorient, Author Collection.

Page 169: The Boulevard Theater today, photo by Daniel J. Berks. Used by permission.

Page 169: 2006 Theater Facade Photo, courtesy of the Marjorie Fust Delin family collection. Used by permission.

Page 169: Galerie Cinema Exterior—Photo Credit Ulrich von Born, reproduced in compliance with Fair Use for commentary and education.

Page 169: Galerie Cinema Interior—Photo Credit Remo Bodo Tietz, reproduced in compliance with Fair Use for commentary and education.

Film advertisements: This book includes reproductions of historical movie advertisements originally published in newspapers over the past 90 years. These advertisements are included under the Fair Use Doctrine of U.S. copyright law (17 U.S.C. § 107). Their use is for purposes of commentary, criticism, scholarship, and historical documentation, all of which are recognized as fair use. Every effort has been made to preserve the original context and intent of these materials as part of the historical record.

Frame Grabs: This book contains copyrighted material, including images and frame grabs from films, used for purposes of commentary, criticism, analysis, and education. These uses are made in accordance with the principles of Fair Use under Section 107 of the Copyright Act of 1976. The materials are used to provide insights into the making and production of films and are included solely to illustrate and support the book's discussion of filmmaking techniques and industry practices. They are not intended to infringe upon the rights of the respective copyright holders. All copyrighted works remain the property of their respective owners. If you believe your copyright has been infringed, please contact the author or publisher to address the matter.

Frame grabs from *Harold and Maude* © 1971, Paramount Pictures. Reproduced in compliance with Fair Use for commentary and education.

Frame grabs from *De Düva,* © 1968, Coe-Davis Limited. Reproduced in compliance with Fair Use for commentary and education.

Frame grabs from *Bambi Meets Godzilla* © 1969, Marv Newland. Reproduced in compliance with Fair Use for commentary and education.

Frame grabs from *Thank You Mask Man* © 1971. Reproduced in compliance with Fair Use for commentary and education.

NOTES

THE WESTGATE BEFORE *HAROLD AND MAUDE* • • • • • • • • • • • • •

The Idea
"The Westgate theater, Morningside's new amusement center …" *The Minneapolis Journal*, November 1935

"In *Lady Tubbs*, Alice Brady comes through handsomely…" *Lady Tubbs* Review, *The New York Times*, July 22, 1935

"Film row was monopolized, so we were unable to get very good pictures…" Marjorie Delin, *Memories of Marjorie Delin*, Edina Historical Society

The Tragedy
"In the fall of 1936, while Daddy was driving …" Marjorie Delin, *Memories of Marjorie Delin*, Edina Historical Society

The War Years and Beyond
"I will never forget when we showed *Gone with the Wind* …" Richard N. Jamieson, *Bridging The Gaps*, Edina Historical Society, 2009

"On one Saturday night at The Westgate …" Ibid

"Theater men have long considered these customers a breed apart …" "Upper Bohemians: A Breed Apart," Will Jones, *Sunday Tribune*, February 22, 1953

"'Mrs. Upper Bohemian …" Ibid

"I used to go to the movies there every Saturday night …" Tippi Hedren's Minneapolis Trip, *Star Tribune*, April 2, 1963

"I hear the recurring complaint that Minneapolis is cheated …" Unusual Films, Don Morrison, *The Minneapolis Star*, June 12, 1969

The Twelve Chairs
"It was an overlooked Mel Brooks movie …" William (Randy) Greene, personal interview by the author, 2024

"*The Twelve Chairs* is a comedy for Brooks watchers …" Vincent Canby, *The New York Times*, October 29, 1970

"*The Twelve Chairs* is the sort of movie that improves …" Roger Ebert, *Chicago Sun-Times*, December 22, 1970

"As preposterous and as much fun as a Roadrunner cartoon …" Don Morrison, *The Minneapolis Star*, January 15, 1971

"Brooks (who plays a drunken servant in the show) …" Ibid

"Mel Brooks has provided The Westgate Theater …" Will Jones, *Minneapolis Tribune*, February 1, 1971

Where's Poppa
"The first film to be dropped from the bunch …" Bern Kerns, *Star Tribune*, January 10, 1971

"About a month after *The Producers* opened …" Roger Ebert, *Chicago Sun-Times*, December 29, 1970

"Because it looks a lot more cruel than it really is …" Vincent Canby, *The New York Times*, December 6, 1970

"Played horribly when the first opened up …." MUBI Podcast: *Harold and Maude* Find New Life, July 14, 2022

"I think they correctly sussed out that there was an appetite …" Ibid

"*Where's Poppa?* keeps staying on and on at The Westgate …" Will Jones, *Minneapolis Tribune*, June 26, 1971

HAROLD AND MAUDE BEFORE THE WESTGATE

The Screenwriter
"'In exchange for light chauffeuring duties ...'" Colin Higgins Interview, The American Film Institute Seminar, 1979

"Colin gave me the impression of being ..." Meeting Colin Higgins, Colin Higgins Trust, June 7, 2001, Criterion *Harold and Maude* DVD

"You could raise the camera head to nine feet ..." Colin Higgins Interview, Criterion *Harold and Maude* DVD

"And at some point, I came home ..." Meeting Colin Higgins, Colin Higgins Trust, June 7, 2001, Criterion *Harold and Maude* DVD

"Ed was constantly pushing scripts at me ..." Ibid

"I took it to Bob Evans and Peter Bart ..." Ibid

"I'll never forget - I was sitting in the living room ..." Colin Higgins Interview, The American Film Institute Seminar, 1979

The Director
"The script was sold with me as the director ..." Colin Higgins Interview, The American Film Institute Seminar, 1979

"They saw the test and they decided..." Michael Sheldin, *Film Quarterly*, Fall 1972

"They were unimpressed ..." Colin Higgins Interview, The American Film Institute Seminar, 1979

"I remember realizing what an amazingly original voice ..." *Harold And Maude* – An Oral History, Interviews By Cameron Crowe and Andy Fischer

"Early on, Hal was very, very picky ..." *Hal*, Documentary by Amy Scott, 2018

"I went back to Paramount..." Hal Ashby Interview, The American Film Institute, 1978

"I talked to Colin about it and he said yes ..." Ibid

Casting
"That's who he always envisioned in that part ..." *Harold And Maude* – An Oral History, Interviews By Cameron Crowe and Andy Fischer

"There were two women in contention for the Maude role ..." Ibid

"When I read *Harold and Maude*, I thought that part's meant ..." *The Twin Cities Welcomes Ruth Gordon and Bud Cort* (documentary) directed by John Gaspard (1974)

"That doesn't sound like me, ducky..." *My Side*, Ruth Gordon, Harper & Row Publishers, 1976

"I have John Schlesinger to thank for my role ..." Vivian Pickles: Being in *Harold & Maude*, https://www.criterion.com/current/posts/2350-being-in-harold-and-maude

"The script was gorgeous to read ..." *Harold And Maude* – An Oral History, Interviews By Cameron Crowe and Andy Fischer

"Computer date number two, Edith Fern ..." Nick Dawson and Charles Mulvehill Commentary, Criterion *Harold and Maude* DVD

"(Shari Summer's) manager had taken her to William Morris ..." *Harold and Maude* at 50 – An Oral History of How a 'Harrowing' Flop Became a Beloved Cult Classic, *Variety*, December 10, 2021

"And it was all her own wardrobe ..." Nick Dawson and Charles Mulvehill Commentary, Criterion *Harold and Maude* DVD

"We tested a lot of people for Harold ..." Ibid

"It's sort of well-known that Bud was not my first ..." Colin Higgins Interview, The American Film Institute Seminar, 1979

Notes

"Colin and I met and knew each other at UCLA …" John Rubinstein, Emails To Author, 2024

"Colin knew that I would interpret the words …" *Harold And Maude* – An Oral History, Interviews By Cameron Crowe and Andy Fischer

"Johnny had done it absolutely the way …" Colin Higgins Interview, The American Film Institute Seminar, 1979

"I wanted an actor who, of course, looked young enough …" Hal Ashby Interview, The American Film Institute, 1978

"All the tests were shot at Hal Ashby's house …" *My Side*, Ruth Gordon, Harper & Row Publishers, 1976

"I walked into this room and Hal …" Bud Cort: 'Harold and Maude was a blessing and a curse,' Alex Godfrey, The Guardian, 10 Jul 2014

"I was very disappointed, not getting Harold and Maude …" *Harold And Maude* – An Oral History, Interviews By Cameron Crowe and Andy Fischer

"But I absolutely *loved* the finished version …" John Rubinstein, Emails To Author, 2024

"I think Hal made the right choice …" Colin Higgins Interview, The American Film Institute Seminar, 1979

Production

"He didn't talk to them from the day we started …" *Harold And Maude* – An Oral History, Interviews By Cameron Crowe and Andy Fischer

"All the interiors and exteriors of the mansion …" Nick Dawson and Charles Mulvehill Commentary, Criterion *Harold and Maude* DVD

"A marvelous place. We only had it for a week …" Vivian Pickles: Being in *Harold & Maude*, https://www.criterion.com/current/posts/2350-being-in-harold-and-maude

"It was this wonderful old mansion that was empty …" *Harold and Maude* at 50 – An Oral History of How a 'Harrowing' Flop Became a Beloved Cult Classic, *Variety*, December 10, 2021

"We see Maude's main room filled with all kinds of eccentric …" *Harold and Maude*, Screenplay by Colin Higgins

"We were meeting Art Directors, and the first question …" *Harold And Maude* – An Oral History, Interviews By Cameron Crowe and Andy Fischer

"The thing about the railroad car …" Ibid

"We had the great idea of parking it on a siding …" Nick Dawson and Charles Mulvehill Commentary, Criterion *Harold and Maude* DVD

"Most (directors) at that time, they would say …" *Harold And Maude* – An Oral History, Interviews By Cameron Crowe and Andy Fischer

"I can still remember this, I can hear him go …" Ibid

"I was an emotional minefield …" *Being Hal Ashby*, Nick Dawson, The University Press of Kentucky 2009

"Hal was so inspiring, with a most wonderful, genuine …" Vivian Pickles: Being in *Harold & Maude*, https://www.criterion.com/current/posts/2350-being-in-harold-and-maude

"Bill Theis, our costume designer, came up with this idea …" Nick Dawson and Charles Mulvehill Commentary, Criterion *Harold and Maude* DVD

"I remember once, it was just a gorgeous sunset …" Bud Cort and John Alonzo Interview, Colin Higgins Trust, February 5, 1997

Happy (and Not So Happy) Accidents

"Was only one dark spot in the movie …" *Harold And Maude* – An Oral History, Interviews By Cameron Crowe and Andy Fischer

"I've seen the piece of film …" Ibid

"Luckily he wasn't seriously hurt …" *Harold and Maude* at 50 – An Oral History of How a 'Harrowing' Flop Became a Beloved Cult Classic, *Variety*, December 10, 2021

"One of the funniest things that ever happened …" Hal Ashby, Dialogue on Film, *American Film Magazine*, May 1980

"It was sort of last minute. Chuck Mulvehill, Hal and I …" *Harold And Maude* – An Oral History, Interviews By Cameron Crowe and Andy Fischer

"One of Hal's strong suits was to be able to …" Nick Dawson and Charles Mulvehill Commentary, Criterion *Harold and Maude* DVD

"(Production Designer) Michael Haller's father had just passed …" Ibid

"I slipped on this marble floor …" *Harold And Maude* – An Oral History, Interviews By Cameron Crowe and Andy Fischer

"Like when we did the scene with Vivian Pickles …" The Colin Higgins Estate

"In the canon of great looks to camera …" Edgar Wright, 90 Minutes Or Less Film Fest: End of 2023 Special with Edgar Wright, Dec 30, 2023

"We had like five cameras …" Nick Dawson and Charles Mulvehill Commentary, Criterion *Harold and Maude* DVD

"So, we have this cheesy stop frame …" Ibid

Post-Production

"Hal shot a lot of film …" *Harold And Maude* – An Oral History, Interviews By Cameron Crowe and Andy Fischer

"I have a tendency, when shooting a lot of film …" Hal Ashby Interview, The American Film Institute, 1978

"The first assembly of the film was three hours long …" Nick Dawson and Charles Mulvehill Commentary, Criterion *Harold and Maude* DVD

"The script was overwritten …" Hal Ashby Interview, The American Film Institute, 1978

"Maude and Harold have just finished planting the tree …" *Harold and Maude*, Screenplay by Colin Higgins

"We took an hour and a half out of the film …" Nick Dawson and Charles Mulvehill Commentary, Criterion *Harold and Maude* DVD

The Music

"Hal loved the script but couldn't figure out …" *Harold and Maude* at 50 – An Oral History of How a 'Harrowing' Flop Became a Beloved Cult Classic, *Variety*, December 10, 2021

"The music plays a big part in any of my films …" Hal Ashby, Dialogue on Film, *American Film Magazine*, May 1980

"What I always used to tell the guys …" Hal Ashby Interview, The American Film Institute, 1978

"I was a little bit cautious …" Yusuf Interview, Criterion *Harold and Maude* DVD

"I always intended to do those songs properly …" *Hal*, Documentary by Amy Scott, 2018

"I never really got that (Cat) Stevens' contribution …" Colin Higgins Interview, The American Film Institute Seminar, 1979

The Preview

"We previewed in Palo Alto, near Stanford …" *Harold And Maude* – An Oral History. Interviews By Cameron Crowe and Andy Fischer

"I sat there, watching the film for the first time …" Shoot Out: Surviving Fame and (Mis)Fortune in Hollywood, By Peter Bart & Peter Gruber, G.P. Putnam's Sons, 2002

"This movie previewed great …" Nick Dawson and Charles Mulvehill Commentary, Criterion *Harold and Maude* DVD

"I had two feelings leaving that screening …" *Harold And Maude* – An Oral History, Interviews By Cameron Crowe and Andy Fischer

The Marketing

"I love that the poster to *Harold and Maude* was just …" *Hal*, Documentary by Amy Scott, 2018

"If you've ever seen the original poster for *Harold and Maude* …" Colin Higgins Interview, The American Film Institute Seminar, 1979

"I think they got some grade school student …" *Harold And Maude* – An Oral History, Interviews By Cameron Crowe and Andy Fischer

"We had the worst campaign in the history …" Ibid

"Nobody knew what to do or how to sell this movie …" Nick Dawson and Charles Mulvehill Commentary, Criterion *Harold and Maude* DVD

"The trailer that I did, Bob Evans hated it …" *Harold And Maude* – An Oral History, Interviews By Cameron Crowe and Andy Fischer

"Pablo and I were kind of surprised …" *Hal*, Documentary by Amy Scott, 2018

"The advertising people at Paramount had no idea …" *Shoot Out: Surviving Fame and (Mis)Fortune in Hollywood*, By Peter Bart & Peter Gruber, G.P. Putnam's Sons, 2002

The Reviews

"It opened and closed in a week …" *Being Hal Ashby*, Nick Dawson, The University Press of Kentucky 2009

"You couldn't drag people in." Bud Cort: '*Harold and Maude* was a blessing and a curse,' Alex Godfrey, *The Guardian*, Thu 10 Jul 2014

"We thought it was a great film …" *Harold and Maude* at 50 – An Oral History of How a 'Harrowing' Flop Became a Beloved Cult Classic, *Variety*, December 10, 2021

"We opened at the Village Theater in Westwood at Christmas …" Colin Higgins Interview, The American Film Institute Seminar, 1979

"I'll never forget, the first review was in *Variety* …" *Harold And Maude* – An Oral History, Interviews By Cameron Crowe and Andy Fischer

"Death can be as funny as most things in life …" Roger Ebert, *Chicago Sun-Times*, January 1, 1972

"Stylish, nutty, enjoyable and oddly provocative …" *Being Hal Ashby*, Nick Dawson, The University Press of Kentucky 2009

"It's a joy. An enchanting excursion into the joy of living …" Judith Crist, *New York Magazine*, December 20, 1971

"You might well want to miss Hal Ashby's *Harold and Maude* …" Vincent Canby, *The New York Times*, Dec 21, 1971

"*Dear Mr. Canby, What a disappointment to read* …" *My Side*, Ruth Gordon, Harper & Row Publishers, 1976

"*Harold and Maude* is a glorious addition to a class of movies …" Don Morrison, *The Minneapolis Star*, Wednesday, December. 29, 1971

"Ruth Gordon is on-the-button as Maude …" Ben Kern, *Star Tribune*, January 2, 1972

HAROLD AND MAUDE AT THE WESTGATE

The Resurrection
"A 15-minute movie that I've been hoping to see …" Will Jones, *Minneapolis Star Tribune*, March 20, 1972

"Now they're bringing *Harold and Maude* back …" Ibid

"I was not there Wednesday …" William (Randy) Greene, personal interview by the author, 2024

The (Short) Movie Before The Movie
"It was playing with a movie called *The Fox* …" 40th Anniversary Screening *Distance & De Düva (The Dove)* Q&A with Cast and Crew, https://www.youtube.com/watch?v=QjgIv0ozT7c

"About two or three minutes into it, people get it …" William (Randy) Greene, personal interview by the author, 2024

"We took this idea to Paramount …" 40th Anniversary Screening *Distance & De Düva (The Dove)* Q&A with Cast and Crew, https://www.youtube.com/watch?v=QjgIv0ozT7c

"And so, the luck of the draw …" Ibid

"It's just interesting, how when you have a vision …" Ibid

Year One
"In the beginning, the younger people were coming …" William (Randy) Greene, personal interview by the author, 2024

"The attendance during the first year ran in cycles …" Daisies For Ruth Gordon, Don Morrison, *The Minneapolis Star*, Friday, March 23, 1973

"We did take surveys once in a while about who …" William (Randy) Greene, personal interview by the author, 2024

"He could count on the fingers of his two hands …" Peg Meier, *Star Tribune*, January 2, 1974

"The *Harold and Maude* success story …" Movie Ad, *Detroit Free Press*, September 29, 1972

The Super Fan: Doug Strand
"It just hit me. I kept going back." Peg Meier, *Star Tribune*, January 2, 1974

"I went back because I was friends …" Doug Strand, personal interview by the author, 2024

"Similarities between us and Harold and Maude …" Peg Meier, *Star Tribune*, January 2, 1974

"It kind of became addictive …" Doug Strand, personal interview by the author, 2024

"When Harold pretends to shoot himself …" Ibid

"When Maude 'borrows' a truck to transport a sickly …" Peg Meier, *Star Tribune*, January 2, 1974

"I saw her a lot …" Doug Strand, personal interview by the author, 2024

"I drove to New York to see that play …" Ibid

"What you saw on TV, what you saw in movies …" Ibid

The One-Year Anniversary
"Somebody from General Cinema called me …" Doug Strand, personal interview by the author, 2024

"Studio biggies had scoffed at the idea …" Maude Is Coming To Town, Don Morrison, *The Minneapolis Star*, March 19, 1973

"Certainly has earned the co-slicer role." Ibid

"I made a lot of preparation to meet her …" Doug Strand, personal interview by the author, 2024

"We didn't have advanced tickets …" William (Randy) Greene, personal interview by the author, 2024

"I arrived at 6:30 p.m. to avoid the last-minute …" Daisies For Ruth Gordon, Don Morrison, *The Minneapolis Star*, Friday, March 23, 1973

"When the tiny, 5-foot star arrived …" Ibid

"After the patrons were more or less seated …" Ibid

"She mounted the stage and in a cracked voice …" Ibid

"When fans suggest that she has perhaps become …" Will Jones, *Minneapolis Star Tribune*, March 25, 1973

"The crowd was half full at the most …" William (Randy) Greene, personal interview by the author, 2024

"I'm still sailing on clouds toward Never-Never Land …" Ruth Gordon Telegram to General Cinema Corporation, 1973

Year Two

"The end is nowhere in sight." Irv Letofsky, *Minneapolis Tribune*, July 24, 1973

"I'd be totally bananas by now if I didn't." Peg Meier, *Star Tribune*, January 2, 1974

"One of the great practical things about *Harold and Maude* …" Amy Eisenstadt, personal interview by the author, 2024

"I remember discussing it with staff and not knowing why …" MUBI Podcast: Harold and Maude Find New Life, July 14, 2022

"At the 95th week …" Ibid

"It got really chewed up, scratched, and splices …" William (Randy) Greene, personal interview by the author, 2024

The Two-Year Anniversary

"(Bud) is strongly committed to a career …" Harold Chasen is in town. THE Harold Chasen, Irv Letofsky, *Star Tribune*, March 30, 1974

"The ruckus came about…" Nancy Livingston, *St. Paul Dispatch*, March 21, 1974

"Well, to hell with him, I thought!" *The Twin Cities Welcomes Ruth Gordon and Bud Cort* (documentary) directed by John Gaspard (1974)

"I'm glad to be here …" Ibid

"I think there's nothing anybody can say …" Ibid

The Protest

"We got a lot of complaints on the phone …" William (Randy) Greene, personal interview by the author, 2024

"A group of Edina residents picketed the Westgate …" Protest Photo, (No Byline), *The Minneapolis Star*, March 21, 1974

"Because there was an occasion and people were going to be there …" Henry Owen, personal interview by the author, 2024

"It wasn't a monumental thing …" Ibid

The End Comes

"After the second anniversary …" MUBI Podcast: Harold and Maude Find New Life, July 14, 2022

"We got so few people for a show …" Amy Eisenstadt, personal interview by the author, 2024

"They announced at the end March …" William (Randy) Greene, personal interview by the author, 2024

"After 114 weeks, two days and $425,000 …" *Harold and Maude* is finally leaving, Irv Letofsky, *Minneapolis Tribune*, May 29, 1974

"At 11:07 p.m. Thursday, a boy named Harold …" Fans give *Harold and Maude* reluctant farewell at Westgate, Bob Lundegaard, *Minneapolis Tribune*, Saturday, June 1, 1974

"'It's the end of an era,' said Douglas Strand …" Ibid

"I was riding around on my motorcycle …" Ibid

"I have a thing about funerals …" Ibid

"She telephoned him last week with some good news …" Ibid

"I couldn't. I didn't have the heart." Ibid

HAROLD AND MAUDE AFTER THE WESTGATE

"They brought it back to the Highland …" Doug Strand, personal interview by the author, 2024

"They've run it here three times in the last year …" What is it about *Harold and Maude*? Lynne Nerenberg, *Twin Cities Reader*, December 16, 1977

"It's an upbeat film that gives an injection …" Ibid

"People just love that movie." Ibid

"Minneapolis is funny …" Tom Shales, *The Montreal Star*, August 10, 1974

"We ship it to college campuses …" After 12 Years, a Profit For *Harold and Maude*, Aljean Harmetz, *The New York Times*, August 8, 1983

"A young man came up to me …" Ibid

"I can walk down the streets of any city …" Harold's Back and Maude's Got Him, Aljean Harmetz, *The New York Times*, May 26, 1974

"Anywhere I've ever gone …" Bud Cort and John Alonzo Interview, Colin Higgins Trust, February 5, 1997

"I thought it was one of those sweepstakes …" After 12 Years, a Profit For *Harold and Maude*, Aljean Harmetz, *The New York Times*, August 8, 1983

"Around 1977, Hal and Ruth and I …" Ibid

"Which theater line could be more suitable for Madeleine Renaud …" Louis Dandrel, *Le Monde*, October 10, 1973

"I took my producers when we were in Paris …" Colin Higgins Interview – Criterion *Harold and Maude* DVD

"Each time it's different …" Ibid

"I got to play Maude and my daughter played …" *Harold and Maude* at 50 – An Oral History of How a 'Harrowing' Flop Became a Beloved Cult Classic, *Variety*, December 10, 2021

"In some remarkable way, Janet Gaynor …" Walter Kerr, *The New York Times*, February 8, 1980

"The play, like the film before it …" Matt Wolf, *The New York Times*, March 8, 2018

"It's impossible, unfortunately, to resist replaying …" Charles Isherwood, *The New York Times*, January 11, 2005

"The subtlety and socially conscious whimsy …" David Rooney, *Variety*, January 10, 2005

"The whole thing rested, quite frankly, on the music …" Harold And Maude – An Oral History: The making of the film and music, as told by the filmmakers and participants, Interviews By Cameron Crowe and Andy Fischer

"It's the music. Boy does that live on …" Ibid

"I refused to allow them to make a soundtrack album …" Yusuf Looks Back on *Harold and Maude*'s Music, Yahoo Entertainment, December 17, 2012

"I was kind of a little bit upset about that …" Yusuf Interview, Criterion *Harold and Maude* DVD

"If I'd never gotten a profit check, it would have been worth it …" After 12 Years, a Profit For *Harold and Maude*, Aljean Harmetz, *The New York Times*, August 8, 1983

THE WESTGATE AFTER *HAROLD AND MAUDE*

The Next Harold and Maude?

"Yeah, they tried. They brought in a foreign film ..." MUBI Podcast: Harold and Maude Find New Life, July 14, 2022

"With *Harold and Maude* finally running out ..." Will Jones, *The Minneapolis Tribune*, May 30, 1974

"Like *Harold and Maude*, which preceded it ..." Bob Lundegaard, *Minneapolis Tribune*, June 4, 1974

"The premise is good, and there are a bunch ..." Roger Ebert, *Chicago Sun-Times*, January 1, 1972

"Isn't a comedy of the highest order ..." Vincent Canby, *The New York Times*, September 23, 1973

"Briskly paced and exceedingly droll." J. Hoberman, *The New York Times*, August 26, 2015

"The only mystery contained in *S*P*Y*S* ..." Nora Sayre, *The New York Times*, June 29, 1974

"Unworthy of anyone's time." *Leonard Maltin's 1996 Movie & Video Guide*, Signet, 1995

"The Westgate Theater, which struck gold a while back ..." Bob Lundegaard, *Minneapolis Tribune*, August 29, 1974

"Sometimes Killing Isn't Humorous." Don Morrison, *Star Tribune*, October 7, 1974

"I attended *Homebodies* in anticipation of a ..." Ibid

King of Hearts

"The people who live near the Westgate Theater ..." Bob Lundegaard, *Minneapolis Tribune*, November 28, 1974

"An "extravagant and highly comic morality play ..." Vincent Canby, *The New York Times*, June 20, 1967

Bambi Meets Godzilla - Thank You Mask Man

"*Bambi Meets Godzilla* was based on my verbal joke ..." Marv Newland, Vantage Point Interviews, https://vantagepointinterviews.com/2021/06/15/godzilla-meets-marv-animator-marv-newland-on-creating-the-classic-short-film-bambi-meets-godzilla/

"Terry Gilliam took me out for lunch ..." Ibid

Meet The New Boss ...

"A General Cinema executive said in a telephone ..." General Cinema will reopen eight movie theaters in Cities, Randy Furst, *The Minneapolis Star*, November 3, 1975

This is The End

"I hesitate to say too much, thus oversell a movie ..." Vincent Canby, *The New York Times*, June 12, 1976

"Livelier than most ..." *Leonard Maltin's 1996 Movie & Video Guide*, Signet, 1995

"The General Cinema Corp. will close four ..." Four General Cinema theaters to close, Bob Lundegaard, *Star Tribune*, July 8, 1977

"Carney is an aging private eye who tries to solve ..." *Leonard Maltin's 1996 Movie & Video Guide*, Signet, 1995

"Benton's nostalgia for the genre works imaginatively ..." Pauline Kael, *The New Yorker*, February 7, 1977

"This one-of-a-kind murder mystery ..." *Pauline Kael, 5001 Nights at the Movies*, Holt, Rinehart and Winston, 1982, 1984

CODA

"In its own small way, *Harold and Maude* ..."
Shoot Out: Surviving Fame and (Mis)Fortune in Hollywood, By Peter Bart & Peter Gruber, G.P. Putnam's Sons, 2002

"I'm looking forward to seeing it again." What is it about *Harold and Maude*? Lynne Nerenberg, *Twin Cities Reader*, December 16, 1977

www.ingramcontent.com/pod-product-compliance
Lightning Source LLC
Chambersburg PA
CBRC101143030426
42337CB00008B/62